THE BOOK THIEF

Markus Zusak

AUTHORED by Justin T. Cass
UPDATED AND REVISED by Damien Chazelle

COVER DESIGN by Table XI Partners LLC
COVER PHOTO by Olivia Verma and © 2005 GradeSaver, LLC

BOOK DESIGN by Table XI Partners LLC

Published by GradeSaver LLC, www.gradesaver.com

First published in the United States of America by GradeSaver LLC. 2009

GRADESAVER, the GradeSaver logo and the phrase "Getting you the grade since 1999" are registered trademarks of GradeSaver, LLC

ISBN 978-1-60259-203-2

Printed in the United States of America

For other products and additional information please visit
http://www.gradesaver.com

Table of Contents

Table of Contents

Biography of Zusak, Markus (1975-)

Born in Sydney, Australia, Markus Zusak began his career writing young adult fiction. The Underdog, Zusak's first novel, was published in 1999 and followed by two sequels, Fighting Ruben Wolfe (2001) and When Dogs Cry (2002). Zusak's 2002 novel The Messenger was well received internationally, winning several awards including a Michael L. Printz Honor selection, a citation given for literary excellence in young adult literature.

In 2006, Zusak's fifth novel The Book Thief was published in his native Australia as the author's first work of "adult" fiction, yet marketed by its American publisher Knopf as another work of young adult fiction. Successful upon publication, over one million copies of The Book Thief have been sold internationally, and the novel received a Printz Honor.

Zusak was born to an Austrian father and a German mother, both of whom experienced World War II firsthand in their native countries. Zusak has stated that The Book Thief was unlike anything he had written before and largely inspired by stories his parents told him as a child about wartime Munich and Vienna. Zusak has specifically singled out two stories his mother told him, one of the bombing of Munich, and one of Jews being marched through Zusak's mother's town on their way to the Dachau concentration camp.

Like The Book Thief's character of Hans Hubermann, Zusak's father was a house painter, and at an early age Zusak wanted to be a house painter as well. Zusak began writing as a teenager, and cited The Old Man and the Sea and What's Eating Gilbert Grape as inspirations. Zusak's sixth novel, a young adult fiction titled Bridge of Clay, is to be published in November 2009.

About The Book Thief

Markus Zusak began his career as a successful writer of young adult fiction, but for his fifth novel, Zusak set out to relate the experiences of his parents growing up during World War II for an adult audience. Zusak has said that much of the inspiration for The Book Thief came from the stories his parents would tell him when he was a child.

Zusak's father, a house painter, was an Austrian who spent the war in Vienna, which in 1945 was besieged and captured by the Soviet Red Army. Zusak's mother was a German who grew up in Munich, where she witnessed firsthand both the intense bombing of that city by Allied planes and the degradation of the Jews during the Holocaust. Of his mother's influence, Zusak has said:

> "Two stories my mother told me affected me a lot. The first was about Munich being bombed, and how the sky was on fire, how everything was red. The second was about something else she saw...

One day, there was a terrible noise coming from the main street of town, and when she ran to see it, she saw that Jewish people were being marched to Dachau, the concentration camp. At the back of the line, there was an old man, totally emaciated, who couldn't keep up. When a teenage boy saw this, he ran inside and brought the man a piece of bread. The man fell to his knees and kissed the boy's ankles and thanked him . . . Soon, a soldier noticed and walked over. He tore the bread from the man's hands and whipped him for taking it. Then he chased the boy and whipped him for giving him the bread in the first place. In one moment, there was great kindness and great cruelty, and I saw it as the perfect story of how humans are." (http://www.randomhouse.com/features/markuszusak/author.html)

Both the bombing of Munich and the Holocaust, as expressed by Zusak's mother, figure strongly in The Book Thief. For example, Death's emphasis on colors as a way of avoiding tragedy contrasts with the horrific and unavoidable redness of a firebombed city. Likewise, the scene of Jews being marched through town with just a singular act of kindness offered to them is a pivotal point in The Book Thief, one which encapsulates the novel's central tension between human kindness and human cruelty.

The Book Thief is also a novel about the power of words. Adolf Hitler and his Nazi Party rose to power in no small part through the sheer power of words, delivered through violent speeches, propaganda, and Hitler's seminal book Mein Kampf. Hitler denounced the Jews, the Communists, and the influence of recent enemies like France as he delivered a message of nationalism, Aryan racial superiority, and the promise that he would remake Germany into a world power that would dominate Europe for the benefit of the German people. In the midst of a worldwide Great

Depression, when the German economy lay in ruins after the nation suffered an embarrassing defeat in World War I, Hitler's message was persuasive -- and dangerous. After coming to power, Hitler pursued a policy of rapid militarization and the systematic extermination of those the Nazis considered to be social undesirables: communists, homosexuals, the disabled, gypsies, Poles, Soviets, opponents to the Nazi regime, and the Jews. Hitler ordered that these people be sent to death camps and murdered, and he used the German state machinery -- from the secret police who sought hidden Jews, to the conductors who drove the trains, to the guards who oversaw the concentration camps -- to achieve this end.

In the 1930s and 1940s, the German people were not necessarily intent on murdering millions of Jews and others. Yet Hitler's sheer persuasiveness, along with his total control of Germany's police and media, compelled average Germans to go along with the Holocaust. The Book Thief emphasizes both the danger of words and their potential redemptive value. On Hitler's birthday, Liesel Meminger defies the Nazis and steals a smoldering book from a public burning of banned literature. Her friend, the Jewish refugee Max Vandenburg, hides the map and key to a safe house in a copy of Mein Kampf. Later, Max rips out pages from the book, washes them in white paint, and draws on them a story that is entirely different from the virulent anti-Jew material that Hitler originally wrote. The Book Thief illustrates that just as words can impel human beings to commit horrific atrocities, words can counteract this vileness. Words can forge a remarkable friendship between a hidden Jew and a German girl, words can defy the Nazis when Hitler's propaganda is erased, and beauty and kindness are planted on his pages.

The Book Thief was published in 2006 in Zusak's native Australia as a work of adult fiction, but was marketed as a young adult novel by the American publisher Knopf. In just a few years after its initial publication, over a million copies of The Book Thief have been sold. In 2007 the novel received a Michael L. Printz Honor selection, a citation given for literary excellence in young adult literature.

Character List

Death

A metaphysical being, Death serves as the dryly cynical narrator of *The Book Thief*. Death's duty is to carry away the souls of the recently departed, which it has apparently done for millenia. In its line of work, Death tries to focus on colors as a way of distracting itself from the survivors of those who have died. Liesel's story is one of a handful of survivors' tales that Death remembers; in fact, Death retrieves the actual written autobiography of Liesel's life after the air raid at the end of the novel. Death is "haunted" by humans and unable to reconcile humanity's capacity for evil with humanity's capacity for good.

Liesel Meminger

Introduced by Death as "The Book Thief," Liesel is nine at the beginning of the novel, when her younger brother dies and she is given up by her mother to live with Hans and Rosa Hubermann in the small town of Molching. Liesel is traumatized by her brother's death, but Hans proves to be a calming foster father; with his help, she learns to read and soon finds comfort in the written word. Over the course of the novel, she befriends Max, the Jew who arrives to hide from the Nazis in the Hubermanns' basement, and falls in love with Rudy Steiner, her best friend. Ultimately, Liesel learns the power of words to influence humans to act towards both good and evil as she experiences the beauty and the brutality of humanity. Death describes her as a "perpetual survivor," and Liesel survives Hitler's reign while many of those whom she loves perish as a result of World War II and the Holocaust.

Max Vandenburg

A 23-year-old Jew who hides from the Nazis in the Hubermanns' basement. Max was a fist-fighter growing up, and as a teenager he resolves not to die without a fight. Max is wracked with anguish and guilt over leaving his family to save himself, but he comes to befriend Liesel as the two share their respective nightmares. Their friendship grows very deep, and Liesel reads to Max every night when he falls comatose. Max makes two books for Liesel, both of which involve thinly-veiled allegories about their friendship and Nazi Germany: an illustrated story called "The Standover Man," and a long book of sketches that includes the short story "The Word Shaker." Max leaves the house after Hans gives an old Jew being marched to a concentration camp a piece of bread in public. Liesel later sees him among such a procession, on his way to Dachau. Max survives the camp, however, and reunites with Liesel shortly after the war's end.

Hans Hubermann

Liesel's silver-eyed foster father. An amateur accordion player, Hans is a tall, gentle man with a remarkable amount of integrity and bravery -- Hans' compassion sets a strong example for Liesel, who is soothed by his presence. His life was saved by a Jew Erik Vandenberg in World War I, and he keeps his promise to Erik's widow by hiding her son Max from the Nazis. A skilled house painter by trade, Hans is horrified by the Nazis' persecution of the Jews, and he brings scrutiny to himself by painting over anti-Semitic slurs on Jewish-owned homes and businesses. Hans' impulsive kindness ultimately gets him in trouble, and he is conscripted to serve in a dangerous air raid recovery unit. Hans survives this assignment, but ultimately dies in the air raid that hits Molching at the end of the novel.

Rosa Hubermann

Hans' wife and Liesel's foster mother. A squat woman who makes some money doing laundry for wealthy neighbors, Rosa has a fiery attitude and frequently employs profanity, especially towards those whom she loves. Death describes Rosa as a good woman for a crisis: she maintains order in the household through difficult times, but her spirit is steadily beat down by several the events in the novel, e.g. Max's illness, Hans' conscription, and the air raids.

Rudy Steiner

Liesel's best friend. One of five Steiner children, Rudy is gallant and impetuous -- he is best known for painting his face black and running around a track imitating Jesse Owens. Rudy is motivated throughout the novel by his love for Liesel; at one point he retrieves Liesel's book from the icy cold river and asks her for a kiss. By the end of the novel, Liesel has come to love Rudy as well; Rudy dies in air raid at the end of the novel, and Liesel kisses his corpse.

Ilsa Hermann

The mayor's wife. An intelligent woman with her own library, Ilsa has spent decades mourning the death of her son Johann, who froze to death in 1918, the final year of World War I. Ilsa takes a liking to Liesel: she witnesses Liesel stealing a book from the book burning and invites Liesel into her home library to read. Ilsa gives Liesel a blank book and encourages her to write, and not to live the rest of her life in despair. Ilsa and her husband take Liesel into their home after Hans and Rosa are killed.

Werner Meminger

Liesel's six-year-old brother who dies at the beginning of the book. Liesel is haunted by the memory of Werner and consistently experiences nightmares about his death for months after arriving in Molching. At one point, Liesel thinks to herself that in her mind, Werner will be six years old forever.

Paula Meminger

Liesel's mother, who gives her up for adoption by the Hubermann's at the beginning of the novel. Liesel's father was taken away by the Nazis for being a Communist, and Paula meets the same fate. As Liesel comes to realize, by giving her daughter away, Paula saves her from persecution.

Tommy Muller

A friend and classmate of Liesel's. Described as a twitchy kid, Tommy has hearing problems due to a chronic ear infection. Tommy is generally helpless and relies on the support of his friend Rudy Steiner.

Frau Diller

The very pro-Nazi shopkeeper who refuses service to anyone who does not salute and say "Heil Hitler" upon entering her corner store.

Frau Holtzapfel

A neighbor of the Hubermanns who has feuded with Rosa for a long time, spitting on the Hubermanns' door on a daily basis. Frau Holtzapfel agrees to stop this practice if Liesel will read to her on a regular basis. She has two sons serving in the German Army in Russia, Michael and Robert. Robert dies at the Battle of Stalingrad, and Michael returns with a bloodied hand. Frau Holtzapfel is emotionally ruined by the death of one of her sons, and after Michael commits suicide, she quietly awaits Death.

Hans Junior

Hans and Rosa's only son. Indoctrinated by Nazi propaganda, Hans Jr. is ashamed of his father's kindness towards the Jews and accuses him of being a coward for not supporting Hitler. He serves in the German Army in Russia and stops returning home for holidays because of his animosity towards his father. Another soldier, Michael Holtzapfel, tells Rosa that he heard that Hans Jr. is still alive, but no other indication is given about Hans Junior's ultimate fate.

Trudy Hubermann

Hans and Rosa's adult daughter.

Franz Deutscher

The Hitler Youth leader described as a sadist by Rudy. At one point, Franz viciously beats Rudy up in the street for throwing a rock at his head.

Erik Vandenburg

Max's father who served in World War I with Hans. Erik saves Hans' life by volunteering him for a writing assignment on the day he and everyone else in his regiment are killed in battle. Erik's death comes at Max is very young. Erik taught Hans to play the accordion, and Hans' accordion was originally Erik's.

Arthur Berg

The fifteen-year-old leader of a small group of thieves. The group mainly steals food from farms, and Arthur is very kind to the others, divvying up their gains fairly and sharing with everyone the food brought to him by Rudy and Liesel. Arthur gives the two a bag of chestnuts before leaving town. He is replaced as leader by a new boy, Viktor Chemmel.

Viktor Chemmel

After Arthur Berg, the second leader of a group of thieves. Unlike Arthur, Viktor is wealthy and steals for excitement. Also unlike Arthur, Viktor is very domineering and cruel to the others; he savagely beats Rudy for his insolence. Viktor is the one who throws Liesel's book into the freezing cold Amper River.

Walter Kugler

Max's best friend. Walter and Max began as fighting partners growing up, but soon became friends. In the early stages of the Holocaust, Walter helps Max hide from the Nazis and arranges for Max to stay at Hans Hubermann's.

Frau Heinrich

Woman from the foster care agency who facilitates the transfer of Liesel to the Hubermanns.

Pfiffikus

An ornery old man with a habit of whistling.

Sister Maria

One of Liesel's teachers, a nun who delivers corporal punishment to insolent students.

Ludwig Schmeikl

A classmate of Liesel's. Ludwig taunts Liesel for not being able to read, and Liesel beats him up. Ludwig is injured at the book burning, and Liesel helps him get away from the crowd, then apologizes for attacking him.

Andy Schmeikl

Ludwig's older brother.

Heinz Hermann

Mayor of Molching and Ilsa's husband.

Johann Hermann

Ilsa's son who froze to death in 1918, presumably while fighting in World War I.

Fritz Hammer

An older boy who introduces Liesel and Rudy to the gang of thieves when Arthur Berg was their leader.

Otto Sturm

A classmate of Liesel's who delivers food to the church every week. Liesel and Rudy knock him off his bicycle and rob him.

Stephan Schneider

Hans' Sergeant in World War I.

Thomas Mamer

A shop owner who catches Rudy for trying to steal a potato and threatens to call the police, but lets him go when he is convinced of how poor Rudy is.

Kurt Steiner

Rudy's older brother.

Barbara Steiner

Rudy's mother.

Alex Steiner

Rudy's father, a tailor who does not hate the Jews, but was somewhat relieved when the Jewish tailors competing with him were driven out of town. Alex refuses to let Rudy be inducted into an Army training academy and is punished with conscription. After the war, Alex, who has lost his entire family in a bombing raid, reopens his store and is kept company by Liesel.

Boris Schipper

Sergeant of the Air Raid Special Unit, of which Hans becomes a member.

Reinhold Zucker

A 23-year-old member of Hans' Air Raid Special Unit. Described as an arrogant hothead and a poor gambler, he accuses Hans of cheating at cards. Later, on a truck, he demands that Hans switch seats with him; when the truck crashes, Reinhold is dead.

Michael Holtzapfel

One of Frau Holtzapfel's sons, Michael served in the German Army in the Battle of Stalingrad, where his hand was severely wounded. At a makeshift hospital, he sees his brother Robert die. He returns home and later commits suicide, unable to live with the guilt of having lived while his brother died.

Robert Holtzapfel

One of Frau Holtzapfel's sons. Robert's legs are blown off at the Battle of Stalingrad, and he dies in a makeshift hospital with his brother Michael by his side.

Adolf Hitler

Historical Fuhrer of Nazi Germany. While not a character in the novel per se, Hitler's propaganda and its consequences -- the war, the Holocaust -- functions as the novel's central antagonist.

Major Themes

Words and Propaganda

Liesel learns throughout the course of the novel that words hold a remarkable power to compel people to commit acts of cruelty. At age 9, Liesel is illiterate, and the first book she learns to read is a manual about grave digging. Learning to read brings Liesel closer to the understanding that Hitler's propaganda is the root of his power and the reason why her mother, father, and brother are dead. Max, who understands well the effect Hitler's propaganda has had on his race, helps impart this lesson through his allegorical story "The Word Shaker." The story describes Hitler's use of oratory to brainwash Germany and compel German citizens to turn against the Jews; a young girl who understands the power of words is capable of defying the Fuhrer through words of compassion and love. Reading -- particularly reading Max's writings to her -- brings Liesel great joy throughout the novel, yet she despairs after seeing Max on his way to a concentration camp, and rips up a book, wondering what good words are. Ilsa gives Liesel a blank book and encourages her to write. Liesel ends up writing the story of her life, ending with the line, "I have hated the words and I have loved them, and I hope I have made them right." This line conveys Liesel's realization of the manipulative power of words and indicates her attempt to master the art of writing for compassionate use, to make words "right."

Thievery

Liesel's thievery is a form of defiance and self-actualization. By stealing a book from a book burning, she defies Nazi censorship and takes her education into her own hands. When Ilsa offers Liesel a book, Liesel refuses it because she is enraged at Ilsa for firing Liesel's foster mother Rosa. Instead, Liesel breaks into Ilsa's home and steals the same book, later stealing others. Ilsa realizes what Liesel has done and is amused by it; she "helps" Liesel steal from her library by leaving her window open and placing books in visible locations. Ilsa is an encouraging figure who desires to help Liesel continue to read, even if it must be on Liesel's terms. Rudy and others steal food because they are hungry, yet Rudy is unable to burglarize a wealthy home despite his anger over the Army having "stolen" his father.

Humanity and Dehumanization

The dehumanization of the Jews was an early stage of the Holocaust. Hitler vilified the Jews, progressively stripped them of their civil rights, and ultimately denied that they were even human -- thus were the Nazis able to try to exterminate the entire Jewish race. Max bitterly remarks that, as a Jew in Nazi Germany, a cold basement is the only place he deserves as he hides from persecution. In Max's fantasies of fighting Hitler, he imagines Hitler propagandizing against him, condemning Max personally as a villain and extreme threat to the German people. The pervasiveness of anti-Semitic Nazi propaganda and the fact that Max is reduced to hiding in his birth country weigh heavily on Max's conscious, and he appears to resign himself to the notion of his own inferiority. Death's cynical narration echoes this sentiment. Max's self-deprecation is probably tied into his feelings of guilt over having left his family to save himself.

Of Hans giving an old Jew being sent to a concentration camp a piece of bread, Death narrates: "If nothing else, the old man would die like a human. Or at least with the thought that he *was* a human. Me? I'm not so sure if that's such a good thing." Death struggles to understand humanity's capacity for both good and evil. Death is stunned both by the murderous Nazis and mankind's irrational taste for war and by the few human beings who exhibit remarkable compassion and strength, like Hans and Liesel. Wondering if the human race is worth anything, Death is torn by this opposition and cannot reconcile it: "I am constantly overestimating and underestimating the human race -- that rarely do I ever simply *estimate* it." Ultimately, Death tells Liesel in the last line of the novel, "I am haunted by humans." It is the capacity of human beings to make different moral choices and the apparent capriciousness of these decisions that haunts Death, which is only capable of a single action.

Cowardice

Hans Junior accuses his father Hans of being a coward for not supporting Hitler, yet in Nazi Germany, it would take much more bravery to defy Hitler and defend the Jews than it would to go along with Nazi ideology. Hans lived through World War I by not going into battle on the day everyone else in his regiment died; he repays Erik, the man who saved his life, by hiding Erik's son Max in his basement during World War II. The punishment for being found with a hidden Jew was certain death. Before the war, Hans brought scrutiny upon him and ruined his business by painting over anti-Semitic slurs written on Jewish-owned houses and shops. When he sees Jews being marched through town on their way to a concentration camp, Hans gives an old Jew a piece of bread and is whipped by a soldier for doing so. After that incident, Hans anticipates the secret police taking him away; when he sees two Nazis wearing black trenchcoats on his street, Hans even runs out and tells them that it's him they want.

Hans regrets giving the Jew a piece of bread because of the potentially disastrous consequences of this deed, but Liesel, impressed by Hans' bravery, tries to reassure him. Liesel and Rudy also give bread to a group of Jews. Later, when Liesel sees Max among a group being sent to Dachau, she defies the Nazi soldiers by latching onto Max and is as well whipped for doing so. These small, individual acts of bravery and defiance in the face of popular Nazi fervor are mostly symbolic. Yet the failure of Germans who doubted Hitler's intentions or were horrified by the Nazis' inhumanity to speak up in the 1930s helped bring about Hitler's rise to power and complete domination of the social, military, and political machinery of the nation. To publicly defy the Nazis after Hitler's rise would require bravery of suicidal proportions.

Abandonment and Survivor's Guilt

In the prologue, Death explains that it is not the dead, but the heartbroken survivors of the dead that it cannot stand to look at. Different characters treat abandonment and guilt in different ways. Michael Holtzapfel survives the Battle of Stalingrad, but is unable to stand his guilt over living when his brother Robert died and ultimately commits suicide. Ilsa Hermann becomes a quiet, sullen woman after her only son is killed in 1918, yet Liesel brings her happiness and she urges Liesel not to make the same mistake she did by suffering for the rest of her life.

In World War I, Hans' friend Erik Vandenberg saves Hans' life by volunteering him for a written assignment on the day everyone in the regiment is sent into battle. Erik dies, and Hans feels guilty over Erik's death because Erik had a young son: Hans transmutes this guilt into a promise to help Erik's widow and ultimately saves the life of Erik's son Max. Max too feels guilty over leaving his family to hide from the Nazis. For him, the price of living "guilt and shame."

Death describes Liesel as the "perpetual survivor": she loses her mother, brother, Hans, Rosa, and Rudy, among others. Liesel is traumatized over the death of her younger brother and the realization that her mother has been persecuted by the Nazis. Liesel initially feels abandoned because her mother gave her up for adoption; she later realizes that her mother did this out of love, to save her daughter's life. After seeing Max be sent to a concentration camp, Liesel is able to turn her despair into writing the story of her own life. At the end of the novel, Death remarks that Liesel has experienced both beauty and brutality, suggesting that Liesel was ultimately able to come to terms with the fact that the human condition necessarily involves both suffering and happiness after having experienced extreme versions of both.

Colors

Death observes colors as a distraction from the anguished survivors of the dead: "I do, however, try to enjoy every color I see--the whole spectrum... It takes the edge off the stress. It helps me relax." In its three encounters with Liesel, Death describes three colors: white, from the snow outside when Liesel's brother died; black, from the night sky when the American pilot crashed his plane; and red, from the sky during the firebombing that took the lives of everyone on Liesel's street. In the prologue, Death conflates these colors into the Nazi flag: a black swastika in a white circle surrounded by a field of red. Death's evasion of human misery draws it to a stark emblem of Nazism, the very cause of that misery within the story. Much like the German people who disagreed with Hitler's violent anti-Semitism, Death tries to look away from atrocities but can only arrive at the cause. Death also tells the reader that it observes "a multitude of shades of intonations," that "a single hour can consist of thousands of different colors." Death's willingness to observe different shades in the color spectrum indicates Death's fundamental indecision about whether the human race is totally good or totally evil, suggesting that in Death's analysis, human beings are at various times capable of being either good or bad.

Hans' Accordion

When Hans dies, Death remarks that Hans' soul is light, because most of it has been put out into other places, including "the breath of an accordion." Liesel writes that the accordion "breathes" when Hans plays and sometimes imagines Hans as an accordion: "When he looks at me and smiles and breathes, I hear the notes." Hans' accordion represents Hans' innate kindness and ability to bring joy to others. Hans does not play the accordion very well, but he does play in a lively manner that people enjoy listening to, and Hans is able to make money playing at a local tavern. When Hans defies the Nazis by painting the homes and businesses of Jews, he is saved from ostracism partly because people like his music. Hans' emotional state is at times expressed through his accordion; when he discovers that Max is in a concentration camp, Hans butchers every song when he tries to play. When Hans is forced to serve in the military, the accordion serves as a stand-in for him; his wife Rosa clings to the accordion at night while Hans is gone. Liesel takes the accordion to Hans' corpse and imagines him playing it; the damaged instrument is the only thing Liesel recovers from the Hubermanns' destroyed home.

The accordion itself was originally owned by Erik Vandenberg, who taught Hans to play when the two served together in World War I and saved Hans' life. After the war, Hans brought the accordion to Erik's widow, who told him to keep it.

Foreshadowing

Foreshadowing is a literary technique in which events that occur later in a story are hinted at in advance. The narrator Death reveals almost all of the crucial events of *The Book Thief* in advance, especially when certain characters die and under what circumstances. In the prologue, Death explains that the novel will include, among other things, "a girl" (Liesel), "an accordionist" (Hans), and "a Jewish fist fighter" (Max). Death also reveals here the bombing raid that takes place at the end of the novel as well as the death of an American fighter pilot; Death describes Liesel as a "perpetual survivor," indicating that she lives through the war while others around her die. *The Book Thief* contains a great deal of foreshadowing: hints and outright revelations about the characters' fates and the outcomes of various events can be found in every part. Zusak's use of this technique keeps the reader's focus on the actual processes by which the characters meet their ends and emphasizes the futility of the characters' individual actions in the face of an all-consuming war.

Glossary of Terms

1346 (Year)

Marks the beginning of the European outbreak of the Plague, which at the time killed somewhere between 75-200 million people, perhaps half of the entire European population

79 (Year)

The year Mount Vesuvius, a volcano in Sicily, erupted, obliterating the Roman cities of Pompeii and Herculaneum and suddenly killing perhaps 10,000

angst

(German) Fear

apfel

(German) Apple

arschgrobbler

(German) Ass-scratcher

arschloch

(German) Asshole

Aryan race

A pseudoscientific categorization of Northern European peoples; the Nazis argued that this race was superior to all others and would dominate the Earth

auch

(German) Also

auf wiedersehen

(German) Goodbye, literally "until we see again"

aufmachen

(German) Open

bahnhof

(German) Train station

bitte

(German) Excuse me; can also mean "you're welcome" or "please"

burgermeister

(German) Mayor

Dachau concentration camp

An infamous concentration camp where about 32,000 prisoners died in total; while Dachau was not an extermination camp per se, about 30,000 Jews were gassed there

danke schön

(German) The German equivalent of "thank you very much"

Deutschland uber Alles

"Germany Above All," a line in the German national anthem and patriotic slogan

dreckiges

(German) Dirty

Duden Dictionary

A German reference dictionary, first published in 1880, that is generally considered to be the standard of German spelling and pronunciation

dummkopf

(German) Stupid head

elend

(German) Misery

Führer

(German) Leader; exclusively refers to Adolf Hitler

frau

(German) Miss

gelegenheit

(German) Opportunity

Gestapo

The Nazi secret police, which was empowered to find and eliminate those accused of treason or hiding Jews

gottverdammt

(German) God-damn it

Glossary of Terms

grotesquerie

The quality of being grotesque or morbid

gut

(German) Good

heil

(German) Hail; used as a Nazi salutation

herr

(German) Mister

himmel

(German) Heaven; also the name of the street the Hubermans live on

Hochdeutsch

(German) High German, standard German speech (as opposed to Low German, which includes dialects and any non-standard speech)

ja

(German) Yes

Jesse Owens

(1913-1980) Black American athlete and record-breaking runner who achieved worldwide fame after winning four gold medals at the 1936 Summer Olympics in Berlin; Hitler was reportedly embarrassed by the victory of a black athlete, which served to counter Nazi propaganda claiming the superiority of the white "Aryan" race

Juden

(German) Jews

kind

(German) Child

Knoller

A certain pub where Hans Hubermann plays the accordion for money

komm

(German) Come; the form "kommst" means "coming"

Kommunisten

(German) Communists; advocates of the communal ownership of property in a classless and stateless society, an ideal first described in 1848 by Karl Marx and Friedrich Engels; the Soviet Union, with which Nazi Germany was at war from 1941 onward, was a nominally Communist nation, and German Communists were persecuted nearly as badly as the Jews by the Nazis

Kristallnacht

(German) "Crystal night"; a coordinated nationwide attack on all Jews in Germany involving lynchings and mob violence against Jews; so called because of the broken glass of shops owned by Jews

lovelily

In a lovely manner

Luft Schutz Raum (LSR)

(German) Air-Raid Shelter

Luftschutzwart

(German) Air-raid supervisor, generally charged with keeping order in a bomb shelter

maler

(German) Painter

Mein Kampf

(German) "My Struggle"; a book written by Adolf Hitler in which he outlines the views of the Nazi Party and ferociously attacks Jews

nachtrauern

(German) Regret

nein

(German) No

NSDAP

National Socialist German Workers' Party, the Nazi Party

richtig

(German) Correct

saukarl

(German) An insult meaning "pig"; the masculine form of "saumensch"

Glossary of Terms

saumensch

(German) An insult meaning "pig"; the feminine form of "saukarl"

scheisse

(German) Shit

scheisskopf

(German) Shithead

schimpferei

(German) Scolding

schmunzel

(German) Smile

schneidermeister

(German) Master-tailor

schnell

(German) Hurry, as a command

schweigen

(German) Silence

schwein

(German) Swine

scythe

A long, curved tool used to reap crops or cut down grass; popular depictions of Death usually include one

sehr

(German) Very

seig

(German) Victory; when combined with "heil," a Nazi rallying call typically accompanied with the Nazi salute, which is the extension of one's right arm at a 45-degree angle, palm down

sickle

Similar to a scythe, an agricultural tool used to reap or mow; in contrast to a scythe, the blade of a sickle is a curved hook; some depictions of Death include one

strasse
(German) Street

und
(German) And

verstehst
(German) Understand, in the 2nd person

verzeihung
(German) Forgiveness

warte
(German) Wait

watschen
(German) A beating

Weihnachten
(German) Christmas

wort
(German) Word

zufriedenheit
(German) Happiness

Glossary of Terms

Short Summary

Narrated by Death, *The Book Thief* is the story of Liesel Meminger, a nine-year-old German girl who given up by her mother to live with Hans and Rosa Hubermann in the small town of Molching in 1939, shortly before World War II. On their way to Molching, Liesel's younger brother Werner dies, and she is traumatized, experiencing nightmares about him for months. Hans is a gentle man who brings her comfort and helps her learn to read, starting with a book Liesel took from the cemetery where her brother was buried. Liesel befriends a neighborhood boy, Rudy Steiner, who falls in love with her. At a book burning, Liesel realizes that her father was persecuted for being a Communist, and that her mother was likely killed by the Nazis for the same crime. She is seen stealing a book from the burning by the mayor's wife Ilsa Hermann, who later invites Liesel to read in her library.

Keeping a promise he made to the man who saved his life, Hans agrees to hide a Jew named Max Vandenberg in his basement. Liesel and Max become close friends, and Max writes Liesel two stories about their friendship, both of which are reproduced in the novel. When Hans publicly gives bread to an old Jew being sent to a concentration camp, Max must leave, and Hans is drafted into the military at a time when air raids over major German cities were escalating in terms of frequency and fatality. Liesel next sees Max being marched towards the concentration camp at Dachau. Liesel loses hope and begins to disdain the written word, having learnt that Hitler's propaganda is to blame for the war and the Holocaust and the death of her biological family, but Ilsa encourages her to write. Liesel writes the story of her life in the Hubermanns' basement, where she miraculously survives an air raid that kills Hans, Rosa, Rudy, and everyone else on her block. Liesel survives the war, as does Max. She goes on to live a long life and dies at an old age.

Quotes and Analysis

"I have hated the words and I have loved them, and I hope I have made them right."
the last line written by Liesel Meminger in her novel "The Book Thief," p. 528

After encountering Max being forced on the way to a concentration camp, Liesel becomes hopeless and disdainful of the written word, seeing Hitler's words as the source of her suffering. Ilsa Hermann gives her a blank book and encourages her to write; Liesel writes the story of her life, containing both tragedy and beauty, at a fevered pace. Liesel has come to the realization that words can cause both violence and comfort, and she strives to make them "right" by combating vicious propaganda with writing that emanates from selflessness and love.

"You want to know what I truly look like? I'll help you out. Find yourself a mirror while I continue."

Death, p. 307

Far from being a Grim Reaper-like representation, *The Book Thief*'s Death is a weary and cynical character with the relatively menial duty of carrying away the souls of the recently deceased. Yet Death's job is made more difficult by the sheer number of people who die by the hands of others in World War II -- Death seems to agonize most over the gas chambers, literal killing machines at Nazi death camps. Death thus takes a skeptical view of war and humanity itself, believing humanity to be capable of tremendous and irrational evils.

"Sometimes I imagined how everything looked above those clouds, knowing without question that the sun was blond, and the endless atmosphere was a giant blue eye."

Death, p. 350

Carrying souls from the gas chamber in Auschwitz, Death imagines the composition of the sky beyond the rain clouds that cover the death camp. In the face of remarkable tragedy, Death expresses optimism that beyond the horrors taking place on Earth, there exists a vivid and unquestionable hope. The "giant blue eye" is potentially a watchful and just God, whose sight has been obscured while His Chosen People are being massacred by the Nazis.

"They had no qualms about stealing, but they needed to be told. They liked to be told, and Viktor Chemmel liked to be the teller."

Death's narration, p. 274

After Arthur Berg leaves Molching, Viktor Chemmel takes his place as leader of a small gang of teenage thieves. Unlike Arthur, Viktor is a cruel boy who steals for fun and demands obedience from the others. The notion of desiring to be controlled is allegorical to the German people under Hitler's dictatorship, and this passage suggests the existence of a certain weakness and complacency that leads humans to obey to the worst commands merely for the sake of order.

"Blood leaked from her nose and licked at her lips. Her eyes had blackened. Cuts had opened up and a series of wounds were rising to the surface of her skin. All from words. From Liesel's words."

Death's narration, p. 253

Liesel explodes at Ilsa Hermann, calling her pathetic and telling her to get over the death of her son. She imagines Ilsa's face becoming physically battered by Liesel's cruel invective. Liesel later comes to regret her tirade, as she realizes the power of words to inflict harm on others.

"Mystery bores me. It chores me. I know what happens and so do you. It's the machinations that wheel us there that aggravate, perplex, interest, and astound me."

Death's narration, p. 243

As narrator, Death employs the technique of foreshadowing throughout the novel to reveal, among other things, the fates -- i.e., survival or death -- of individual characters. Just prior to this passage, Death describes how Rudy Steiner dies at the end of the book. Marcus Zusak's employment of foreshadowing places emphasis on the events and "machinations" in Nazi Germany that lead the characters to their ends.

"There were the erased pages of Mein Kampf, gagging, suffocating under the paint as they turned."

Death's narration, p. 237

Max whitewashes pages of Hitler's propaganda book *Mein Kampf* and draws an entirely new story upon them: a brief retelling of his life, his family's persecution by the Nazis, and his friendship with Liesel. Just as Hans used the same copy of *Mein Kampf* to help bring Max to safety, Max boldly transforms Nazi ideology into compassion.

"Did they deserve any better, these people? How many had actively persecuted others, high on the scent of Hitler's gaze, repeating his sentences, his paragraphs,

his opus? Was Rosa Hubermann responsible? The hider of a Jew? Or Hans? Did they all deserve to die? The children?"

Death, p. 375

Death compares the plight of the German civilians cowering in a bomb shelter with the certain death of the Jews trapped in Nazi gas chambers. Death's musings bring up the notion of collective responsibility for Hitler's crimes, and Death wonders how culpable these people are for the ongoing Holocaust. While they are all citizens of a nation in the process of killing millions of innocent people, some, like Rosa and Hans, quietly defy the Nazis by hiding a Jew, while others are defenseless children who cannot possibly be held responsible for crimes planned before they were even born.

"The word shaker and the young man climbed up to the horizontal trunk. They navigated the branches and began to walk. When they looked back, they noticed that the majority of onlookers had started to return to their own places. In there. Out there. In the forest.

But as they walked on, they stopped several times, to listen. They thought they could hear voices and words behind them, on the word shaker's tree.

"

excerpt from Max's story "The Word Shaker," p. 450

In Max's story, Hitler grows a forest of propaganda-bearing trees, yet a young girl ("the word shaker") plants an indestructable tree that grows miles high from a seed of friendship. She stays at the top of the tree until her friend ("the young man") meets her there. When they climb down, the tree falls, smashing a large part of Hitler's forest. They walk down the tree trunk, and although most of the indoctrinated people return to Hitler's forest, others quietly follow the two friends. Despite the violent against Jews in Nazi Germany, there were a number of Germans who disagreed, if only quietly, with Hitler's persecution. Max's story aims to encourage Liesel to be brave and willing to counter words of hatred with words of love; these final lines suggest that others would be willing to follow her if she took such a stand.

"I am haunted by humans."

Death, the last line of the novel, p. 550

The Book Thief is framed by Death's contemplation of the worth of humanity, and Death's inability to reconcile the remarkable cruelty and the remarkable compassion of which human beings are simultaneously capable. Liesel's life story contains elements of both, and by the end of the novel, Death appears to be no more capable

Quotes and Analysis

of judging humanity than at the novel's outset. Thus, Death tells Liesel that it is "haunted" by humans, just as humans are haunted by Death. A jaded metaphysical being so used to dying could only be fearful of -- and, at times, amazed by -- those who live.

Summary and Analysis of Prologue

Death introduces itself as the book's narrator and describes its work: after one dies, Death carries one's soul off from one's corporeal body. Death describes itself as affable, yet not nice; in discussing this work, Death is candid, noting that the reader is going to die, but that this is "nothing if not fair." In the prologue, Death acquires a cynical, sarcastic, and bluntly dark tone in addressing the audience and describing its work. Throughout the rest of the book however, Death's narration is less affected and can best be described as "third person subjective": Death will convey the dramatic events of the story of Liesel Meminger with occasional analysis.

Death explains that it deliberately tries to notice colors -- as opposed to bodies and people -- in its line of work as a way of distracting itself from the survivors, whom Death considers to be more tragic than the actual dead. Death introduces the story of a "perpetual survivor," later identified as Liesel Meminger, and briefly reveals the three episodes in which Death interacts with Liesel. Death thus foreshadows three key events expanded later in the book in the following three parts of the prologue.

BESIDE THE RAILWAY LINE [Described in Part One]

Death describes the blinding white of the snow and paints a small scene of two guards, one mother and daughter, and one corpse on the ground by a stopped train. The guards argue over what to do with the corpse. Death tries to focus on the snow but becomes curious about the girl and instead waits. The girl is described as "the book thief." Although not revealed here, the daughter is Liesel.

THE ECLIPSE [Part Nine]

A plane has crashed, and a boy with a toolbox -- later revealed to be Rudy Steiner -- arrives first at the scene. Liesel, the book thief, arrives next, and even though "years had passed," Death recognizes her. The boy takes a teddy bear out of his toolbox and puts it on the pilot's chest, and a crowd appears. The pilot's face appeared to be smiling; Death calls this a "final dirty joke," "another human punch line." Death carries off the pilot's soul and sees a momentary eclipse. Death says it has seen millions of these while carrying off souls, more than it cares to remember. Although not explained here, the pilot is an American who has just participated in an air raid; the Rudy, Liesel, and the rest of crowd has just come from bomb shelters.

THE FLAG [Part Ten]

Death: "The last time I saw her was red." This is the fiery sky of a massive bombing raid. Death finds piled bodies stuck to the street and rhetorically asks if fate or misfortune glued them there. Sardonically, Death answers its own question: "Let's not be stupid. / It probably had more to do with the hurled bombs, thrown down by humans hiding in the clouds." Death finds the book thief kneeling among rubble, clutching a book. Death wants to console her, but "that is not allowed." Instead Death follows her; she drops the book and Death later takes it from a garbage truck. Death: "I would keep it and view it several thousand times over the years."

Death explains that these three colors -- red, white, black -- most resonate with its memories of Liesel, and draws them on the page as a dash of red, a circle of white, and a swastika for black. These are the colors and symbols of the Nazi flag; the implication is that Nazism is responsible for the deaths in these three episodes.

Finally, Death explains that it carries a small legion of stories of perpetual survivors like Liesel, and that each one is "an attempt -- an immense leap of an attempt -- to prove to me that you, and your human existence, are worth it."

Death cautions the reader that it is not a violent or malevolent entity, that it is instead a "result." On a practical level, death is a biological process, the "result" of the end of a living being's metabolic processes. Yet in the frame of this novel, Death implies that it exists as a result of humanity's actions, that Death is kept busy by men who kill other men. The capacity of men to do evil, along with the capacity of men to do good, is a central theme of The Book Thief, and Death is both fascinated and conflicted by these extremes. Hitler and Stalin represent one extreme, Liesel and Hans Hubermann another. The novel invites the reader to consider the "worth" of humanity along with Death.

Summary and Analysis of Prologue

Summary and Analysis of Part One

Summary

The novel begins in January 1939. Liesel Meminger is 9 years old.

ARRIVAL ON HIMMEL STREET

On a snowy night, the book thief Liesel Meminger and her six-year-old brother Werner are traveling with their mother by train to Munich, where Liesel and her brother are to be given over to foster parents. Half asleep, Liesel dreams of Adolf Hitler speaking at a rally where Hitler smiles at Liesel, and Liesel, who is illiterate, greets him in broken German. As Liesel's mother sleeps, Liesel sees Werner die, and Death takes Werner's spirit but remains to watch what happens next. The train stops due to track work, and the three exit with two guards who argue over what to do with the body.

Two days later, Liesel's brother is buried by two gravediggers. Traumatized, Liesel digs at her brother's grave but is carried away by her mother. Before leaving on another train, Liesel steals a black book from the cemetery ground.

In Munich, Liesel is given to foster care authorities and driven up to Himmel ("Heaven") Street in the small town of Molching. There is the home of Rosa Hubermann, a squat woman with a short temper, and her husband Hans Hubermann, a tall quiet man who rolls his own cigarettes. At first Liesel refuses to get out of the car; only Hans is able to coax her out. Liesel has just a small suitcase containing clothes and the stolen book: *The Grave Digger's Handbook.*

GROWING UP A *SAUMENSCH*

Death remarks that Liesel will steal several books and be made two by a hidden Jew.

Liesel is very malnourished upon arrival. Her father was a Communist, but she does not yet know what this means. Liesel feels abandoned by her mother but dimly understands that she is being "saved" from poverty and persecution. Rosa, described as loving Liesel yet acting harshly, constantly shouts profanity at Liesel, calling her a *saumensch* ("pig girl") when she refuses to have a bath. Hans, described as a house painter and accordion player, acts more kindly, teaching Liesel to roll a cigarette. Liesel begins to call her foster parents "Mama" and "Papa."

THE WOMAN WITH THE IRON FIST

For the first few months, Liesel would have a nightmare about her brother every night and wet the bed. Hans would come in and sit with her. Secretly Liesel keeps *The Grave Digger's Handbook* under her bed; despite not being able to read even the title, Liesel is reminded by it of the last time she saw her brother and mother.

A few regular activities are introduced. Liesel begins school but is forced into a much younger class of students just learning the alphabet. In February Liesel turns ten and is enrolled into the Hitler Youth. Hans goes to a bar some evenings to play the accordion for money. Rosa, who does laundry for wealthier neighbors, takes Liesel on deliveries and privately berates her customers. Rosa forces Liesel to deliver a bag to the mayor's house, where the mayor's wife silently takes it. Frau Holtzapfel, a neighbor feuding Rosa, spits on the Hubermann's door every night, and Liesel is made to clean it.

THE KISS (A Childhood Decision Maker)

Himmel is a relatively poor street. Some of the neighbors include Rudy Steiner, one of six who lives next door to the Hubermanns; Frau Diller, a staunch Aryan cornershop owner; Tommy Muller, a twitchy kid suffering from ear infections; and Pfiffikus, a vulgar man. The neighborhood kids play soccer with garbage cans for goals, and Liesel is made to be goalie (replacing Tommy). Rudy confidently fires a shot, but Liesel blocks it; in response Rudy hits Liesel with a snowball.

Rudy is made to walk Liesel to school, and he takes a liking to her. He explains that Frau Diller is so committed to the Nazi Party that she refuses service to anyone who does not say "heil Hitler" upon entering her shop. They pass Rudy's father's tailor shop, then a street of broken, empty homes labeled with yellow Stars of David. At school, Rudy constantly seeks Liesel out despite others' comments on her supposed stupidity; Rudy is implied to be in love with Liesel. The two race the hundred meters and Rudy bets a kiss on it; they both slip before the finish, but Rudy says that one day Liesel will "be dying to kiss" him.

THE JESSE OWENS INCIDENT

A flashback to 1936, when Jesse Owens, the black American runner, wins four gold medals at the Berlin Olympics, embarrassing Hitler and the racist Nazis. Rudy, obsessed with the achievement, paints himself black with charcoal and runs the 100 meter relay at an empty track, imagining himself to be Owens. Rudy's father Alex Steiner drags his son home and lectures him not to pretend to be black or Jewish because of the Nazis' racial policies. It is noted that Alex is a member of the Nazi Party but not a racist, and that he will do anything to support his family, even if that means being in the party.

THE OTHER SIDE OF SANDPAPER

In May brown-shirted Nazis march through town, and Hans is revealed to not be a supporter of Hitler. After one of Liesel's nightmares, Hans finds her book and agrees to read it to her. Hans, a poor reader himself, is puzzled by the book about grave-digging, but begins reading to the young girl anyway. Hans finds that Liesel cannot read any words herself, so he begins teaching her the alphabet using sandpaper and a painter's pencil.

THE SMELL OF FRIENDSHIP

Hans continues reading to and teaching Liesel every night after her continued nightmares. Hans even accompanies Liesel when Rosa makes her do laundry deliveries. Hans and Liesel begin working in the basement, where they begin using paint on the cement wall for their lessons.

THE HEAVYWEIGHT CHAMPION OF THE SCHOOL-YARD

In September Germany invades Poland, starting World War II. Rationing begins as England and France join the fight against Germany. Liesel is moved up to the same class as Rudy and Tommy, the proper level for her age. All the students but Liesel are made to perform readings; Rudy interjects at the end that Liesel hadn't gone. The teacher, Sister Maria, refuses, but Liesel insists. Liesel cannot read her piece, so she instead begins to recite a chapter from *The Grave Digger's Handbook*, which she memorized from Hans' readings. Sister Maria takes Liesel into the corridor and gives her a *watschen* (beating) as the class laughs.

Later, Liesel is taunted by her classmate Ludwig Schmeikl. Rudy urges her to ignore Ludwig, but she instead savagely beats him. Still enraged, she also punches Tommy a few times and announces to the stunned crowd of students, "I'm not stupid." Back in class, Sister Maria punishes Liesel with a severe *watschen*. On the way home from school, Liesel thinks about her brother's death and the humiliating day, and Rudy comforts her.

Analysis

Liesel's brother's death inspires many of significant events that set the novel's plot in motion. Liesel's obsession with words and learning to read -- a central part of The Book Thief -- is sparked by stealing *The Grave Digger's Handbook*, which to her at first was only a memento. Liesel's trauma and recurring nightmares cause her special closeness with and trust in her foster father Hans, a gentle man who is an extremely calming presence.

The small town of Molching and its cast of characters is the background of the novel, and the apparent quietness and stability of the town becomes steadily consumed by the political events surrounding the Nazis, the Holocaust, and World War II. Some instability is already evident: the broken shops and anti-Jew graffiti are signs of the Holocaust, and the Jews have already been terrorized and driven into concentration camps. Like the Jews, Liesel's father was persecuted and presumably killed or placed in a camp for being a Communist, and her mother gave Liesel up in part so Liesel could avoid the same fate.

While some characters like Frau Diller are staunch Nazis, others like Hans and Alex Steiner are worried about Hitler and the war, yet do not speak up against the steady destruction of their way of life. Death remarks that one gravedigger does what he is told by the other, and wonders what if the "other" is more than one person. This is a metaphor for Nazi Germany, where one man, Hitler, commands the entire nation, which obeys him unquestioningly.

Liesel's senseless brutalization of Ludwig and Tommy is compared with Hitler's invasion of Poland. In his rise to power, Hitler promised to restore Germany's greatness following a humiliating defeat in World War I. Similarly, Liesel "avenges" her humiliation through violence. Liesel later comes to regret this, and eventually realizes the superior power that words hold to violence.

As Liesel's brother died, Liesel was dreaming of listening "contentedly" to the literally glowing stream of words coming from Hitler's mouth. Yet Liesel could not speak well and had no understanding of the evil meaning of these words. Like the majority of the German people, Liesel was attracted in a childlike way to Hitler's oratory; as Liesel learns to read later in the book, she comes to understand the true horror of this. Hitler violently attacked the Jews in his speeches and preached hatred to his followers; Liesel's brother dying while fleeing persecution and poverty is juxtaposed with this.

Summary and Analysis of Part Two

Summary

A GIRL MADE OF DARKNESS

Death explains that Liesel Meminger will steal her second book, *The Shoulder Shrug*, from a book burning on Hitler's birthday and hints at many of the events that follow. Death remarks that Nazi Germany was built in particular on burning: synagogues, houses, Reichstags, and books.

THE JOY OF CIGARETTES

In late 1939 Liesel, despite having nightmares about her dead brother still, has settled into life in Molching. She loves her foster parents Hans and Rosa, her best friend is Rudy Steiner, and her reading and writing is improving. In December Hans finishes reading *The Grave Digger's Handbook* to Liesel.

On Christmas, the Hubermanns' adult children Hans Junior and Trudy visit, and Liesel, not expecting to get anything at all because of the family's lack of money, receives two books: *Faust the Dog* and *The Lighthouse*, the latter written by a woman. Hans traded his precious cigarette rations for them.

THE TOWN WALKER

Rosa loses a laundry customer because the war has forced him to cut back. Rosa forces Liesel to pick up and deliver the laundry, thinking the customers might pity Liesel. One customer, the mayor's wife Frau Hermann, never speaks. In school, Liesel receives an assignment to write a letter to a classmate and decides instead to write to her birth mother. Hans is somewhat disturbed by this and suggests Frau Heinrich from the foster care office can send the letter. Later, Liesel overhears Hans and Rosa discussing her mother, with Rosa asking rhetorically, "Who knows where she is? Who knows what they've done to her?"

DEAD LETTERS

A brief flash forward to September 1943 where Hans tells Liesel that he nearly wrote her a under her mother's name as Liesel writes in a book.

In early 1940 Liesel checks the mail daily but does not receive a response from her mother. Liesel writes several more letters to her mother, but doesn't send them. Rosa loses another customer. On Liesel's birthday she receives no presents, but resolves to take some of the scant ironing money to mail her letters. When Liesel admits to stealing the money, Rosa starts beating her but immediately stops and apologizes when Liesel says that she mailed her letters. Liesel realizes that she will never see her mother again and remains on the kitchen floor, unable to move. She sheds a single yellow tear.

HITLER'S BIRTHDAY, 1940

To celebrate Hitler's birthday, a book burning is prepared in Molching. Propaganda, banned and censored books, and written material from the era between World War I to the rise of the Nazis are collected. Every house puts up a flag, and the Hubermanns panic when they briefly cannot find theirs. The Hubermann children Hans Junior and Trudy arrive. Trudy is a maid in Munich, Hans Junior is a soldier and fanatical Nazi. Hans Senior is not a Nazi, and he blew his chance to join the party for painting over anti-Jewish slurs. The father and son argue fiercely; Hans Junior accuses his father of being disloyal to Germany and asks why Liesel isn't reading Hitler's book *Mein Kampf*. Hans Junior then calls his father a coward for doing nothing while "a whole nation cleans out the garbage and makes itself great" and storms out. Death explains that Hans Junior would end up at the Battle of Stalingrad, where Death was extremely busy carrying the souls of dead soldiers.

100 PURE GERMAN SWEAT

The Hitler Youth divisions march at the book burning then disperse. Carts of banned material are dumped in the town square. Despite her own love of books, Liesel is excited by the prospect of the fire, and Death wonders simply if "humans like to watch a little destruction." A man at a podium gives a violent speech condemning Jews and Communists, and Liesel suddenly makes the connection between Nazism and the fate of her family, as her father was a Communist. As the crowd goes "Heil Hitler!" and the books are set on fire, Liesel becomes nauseated and tries to escape. Death wonders if anyone ever got injured performing a Nazi salute and dryly remarks that no one ever died from it, except for the forty million people Death picked up.

Liesel runs into Ludwig Schmeikl, who has been injured in the crowd. She pulls him away to the steps of the church then apologizes for beating him.

THE GATES OF THIEVERY

Hans meets Liesel at the church steps, and she asks him if her mother is a communist. Hans lies and says he does not know. Liesel asks if Hitler took her mother away, and Hans, finding it impossible to lie, says yes. Liesel says she hates Hitler, and Hans, worried about what to do, slaps her and orders her never to say that again. Hans forces Liesel to do a proper Nazi salute and say "Heil Hitler."

BOOK OF FIRE

Hans leaves Liesel to talk to a friend. Hans admits he is not getting much work as a painter because he is not a member of the Nazi Party. Liesel goes up to the

Summary and Analysis of Part Two

smoldering heap of the book burning as workers cart away ashes. Liesel sees three books that remain mostly intact and she steals a blue book called *The Shoulder Shrug*. She puts it under her shirt even though it is still hot. Although she was ignored by the workmen, Liesel realizes that one person saw her steal the book: the mayor's wife, Frau Hermann.

Hans and Liesel begin to walk home as smoke rises from Liesel's collar.

Analysis

Liesel is shocked by the realization that Hitler is responsible for the death and disappearance of her family, yet Hans forces her to publicly salute the Fuhrer, fearing what would happen if others heard her say she hated Hitler. Unable to admit her true feelings, Liesel boldly commits her first act of defiance against the Nazis by stealing a banned book in public. Here, Liesel's motivation for reading and stealing books evolves from sadness over her brother's death to rebellion and vengeance against Hitler. Liesel's mode of retribution is, however, not violent. Her very first action upon making her realization is to help and make peace with Ludwig, the classmate she savagely attacked earlier. Her immediate response to the hatred espoused by the Nazi speaker is one of friendship.

Hans' character becomes more complex as it is revealed that he is not a member of the Nazi Party, his application having been tabled because of his willingness to paint Jewish homes and cover up Jewish graffiti. As a result, Hans' business suffers despite his talent, his standing in the community becomes threatened despite his affability, and his relationship with his son is ruined despite their former closeness. Hans Junior is fully indoctrinated in Nazi ideology and speaks in broad metaphoric terms of restoring Germany's greatness by eliminating social undesirables -- unbeknownst to him, this would include Liesel. He revolts against his father and says that Hans is part of an "old, decrepit Germany," one which lost World War I and is supposedly being rebuilt and avenged by the Nazis. Ironically, Hans Junior calls his father a coward for privately opposing Hitler and the Nazi platform, yet Hans' willingness to help Jews is much more dangerous than supporting Hitler. The meaning of cowardice and the question of whether or not Hans is a coward is a moral question that is revisited throughout the rest of the novel.

Summary and Analysis of Part Three

Summary

THE WAY HOME

Liesel shows Hans the book she stole from the book burning, *The Shoulder Shrug*. Hans examines it and becomes worried about its content and the political repercussions of Liesel's act. Hans asks Liesel if she will keep a secret for him should he ask, and Liesel promises yes. Later, Hans purchases a copy of *Mein Kampf* from the Nazi Party office and overhears party officials saying that Hans' application to join the party will never be approved.

THE MAYOR'S LIBRARY

Liesel becomes anxious and paranoid because Ilsa Hermann, the mayor's wife, had seen her steal the book. Rosa forces Liesel to deliver laundry to Ilsa's home, and so she goes with Rudy. Liesel is relieved when Ilsa, noticing Rudy, merely takes the laundry and says nothing.

A few weeks later, Liesel returns to the mayor's house to pick up laundry. Unusually, Ilsa beckons Liesel inside. Ilsa brings Liesel into her home library stocked with books. Excited, Liesel runs her hands along the shelves. She helps Ilsa put away a stack of books then awkwardly departs, laundry in hand. On her way home, Liesel wonders why she said nothing to even thank Ilsa for showing her the library and decides to run back. This time the mayor Heinz Hermann answers the door, and Liesel stammers then awkwardly says "thank you" and leaves.

ENTER THE STRUGGLER

The setting changes to Stuttgart, where a starving Jew named Max Vandenburg is hiding alone in a storage room. A friend enters briefly and gives Max some food and a book secretly containing a card, map, key, and directions. The friend promises to return in a few days. Max is to travel to the home of a stranger, Hans Hubermann.

THE ATTRIBUTES OF SUMMER

In the summer of 1940 Liesel and Hans read *The Shoulder Shrug*, a book banned because its protagonist is a Jew. Ilsa begins allowing Liesel to read in her library during deliveries. On one such occasion, Liesel finds the name "Johann Hermann" written on a book cover. Johann was Ilsa's son who died in 1918, the final year of World War I; Ilsa says he froze to death. Ilsa still suffers because of her son's death, and Liesel tells her, "I'm sorry."

Food is scarce for both Rudy and Liesel's families, and one day they see an older boy, Fritz Hammer, eating an apple. They follow him to a group of four boys led by a 15-year-old thief, Arthur Berg. The boys recognize Liesel for beating up Ludwig Schmeikl and Rudy for the Jesse Owens incident. The boys let Liesel and Rudy come along to steal apples and tell them that if they get caught on the guard fence they will be left behind. Afterwards, Rudy and Liesel receive a dozen apples for their work and eat all of them. Liesel vomits later.

THE ARYAN SHOPKEEPER

Rudy and Liesel find a coin on the ground and buy from Frau Diller a single candy, which they take turns sucking on.

THE STRUGGLER, CONTINUED

The story of Max Vandenburg is resumed. Max's friend Walter Kugler returns to the storage room and says he is being shipped out in the army. Walter leaves a ticket and shaving materials. Nervous Max leaves his hiding place and boards a train with the book he was given earlier, *Mein Kampf*.

TRICKSTERS

Rosa loses another laundry customer. Rudy and Liesel steal from more farms with Arthur Berg. One day, Liesel and Rudy rob a classmate named Otto Sturm who, every Friday, delivers goods to the church on his bicycle. Liesel and Rudy knock Otto off his bike and take the package, which contains eggs, bread, and a ham. They take the package to Arthur, who calls the rest of the boys and cooks the food. Liesel and Rudy return the empty basket to Otto. A few days later, Liesel and Rudy go stealing again but are confronted with an ax-wielding farmer. While making their escape, Rudy gets caught on the fence. The rest of the boys run, but Liesel and Arthur go back to help him despite Arthur saying earlier he wouldn't.

Later, Arthur moves to Cologne and gives Liesel and Rudy a bag of chestnuts as a parting gift. Death explains that Arthur lives through the war, but saw him once with his dying sister during a bombing raid.

THE STRUGGLER, CONTINUED

Max finally arrives at the Hubermanns' home.

Analysis

Two important characters are developed in this part: Ilsa Hermann, the mayor's wife, and Max Vandenburg, a hiding Jew who arrives to live with the Hubermanns. Ilsa is a silent and mysterious woman who lives in sorrow over the death of her son. She takes a liking to Liesel and does not turn Liesel in for the political crime of stealing from a book burning, instead inviting Liesel to read from her massive library. It is unclear why the wife of a high ranking local political figure would act in this way, but the fact that her son froze to death at the end of World War I suggests that Ilsa, like Hans Hubermann, privately objects to Hitler and the Nazis' new war. While Max's character is not yet fully introduced, his appearance in this part injects the Holocaust prominently into the novel and adds an element of immediacy and mortal conflict to contrast with Liesel's comparably easy time in Molching in the middle of 1940.

Arthur Berg and his gang of thieves offer Rudy and Liesel another outlet for rebellion. By stealing from farms, they revolt against rationing restrictions and their families' economic circumstances. Arthur at first seems like a shady character, yet proves himself to be very generous and loyal to his fellow thieves. Arthur shows his compassion by helping Rudy flee the ax-wielding farmer despite having said earlier that anyone who is stuck on the fence would be left behind. Arthur Berg represents a glorious depiction of Communism. Arthur, who is poor himself, promotes the equitable redistribution of stolen goods among his comrades and shows a willingness to take the property of those with more food than he. (Note that the name of the boy who leads Liesel and Rudy to the gang is "Fritz Hammer"; the Soviet symbol is a hammer and sickle.) Yet the episode in which Liesel and Rudy steal from Otto Sturm is a surprisingly cruel one, and suggests at the darker side to this thievery. As Otto was delivering food to church, this scene may be a comment on the anti-religious policies of the U.S.S.R. and Marxist doctrine.

Summary and Analysis of Part Three

Summary and Analysis of Part Four

Summary

THE ACCORDIONIST (The Secret Life of Hans Hubermann)

Max is standing in the Hubermanns' kitchen. He asks Hans if he still plays the accordion, and Hans says yes. The rest of this section is a flashback to Hans' past.

Hans was a mediocre 22-year-old soldier fighting in France in World War I. He was not particularly eager to fight. Hans befriends a German Jew named Erik Vandenburg, who teaches Hans to play the accordion. The day the platoom is to go into battle, the Sergeant asks which one of them has good handwriting. None volunteered. The Sergeant says that whichever man does will not be going into battle, yet no man wants to seem like a coward. Erik nominates Hans, who is sent to write letters for the captain. The rest of the men are all killed.

Hans keeps Erik's accordion and tracks down his family to tell them what happened. Hans credits Erik with saving his life. Hans is surprised to find that Erik has a young son named Max. Hans leaves Erik's widow with his name and address and offers to help if they should need anything.

Hans returns to Munich and works as a painter. He and Rosa have two children, Hans Junior and Trudy. In 1933, Hitler comes to power, and Hans thinks that he does not hate the Jews, because a Jew saved his life and many of his customers are Jewish. As the persecution of the Jews picks up, Hans steadily loses business because he is not a member of the Nazi Party. In 1937, Hans applies to join; afterwards he sees a Jew-owned store vandalized and grafittied. Over the owner's objection, Hans offers to repaint the door. Angry over what he has seen, Hans punches through the door and window of the Nazi Party office and tells a member that he cannot join. In 1938, the Jews are cleared out of town and Hans' home is searched by the Gestapo. Luckily, Hans, whose application was added to a waiting list and not formally withdrawn, is allowed to stay. Hans is not ostracized by his neighbor in part because he plays the accordion warmly. In 1939, six months before Liesel's arrival, Hans is approached by a man named Walter Kugler, who asks if Hans likes to keep a promise.

A GOOD GIRL

The scene from earlier resumes. It is November 1940 and Max is 24. Liesel sees Hans and the stranger standing in the kitchen, and Hans tells her to go back to bed. Hans tells Max not to worry about Liesel.

A SHORT HISTORY OF THE JEWISH FIST FIGHTER

This section is a flashback to Max's past. Growing up, Max loved to fight. His father died when he was two. When Max was nine his mother was broke and the two moved in to his uncle's home, with six cousins. At thirteen, Max's uncle died. Watching his uncle die quietly, Max resolved that he would never die without a fight, and says "When death captures me, he will feel my fist on his face." Death comments that it likes that "stupid gallantry."

As a teenager Max continues fighting among a group of friends and enemies. Max fights a kid named Walter Kugler and wins; the two go on to fight thirteen more times, and they become good friends. In 1935, Max loses his job for being a Jew. The Nurmenburg Laws are passed, barring Jews from having German citizenship and marrying Germans. On November 9, 1938, Kristallnacht ("Night of Broken Glass"), Jewish stores and homes across Germany are attacked. Walter provides an opportunity for Max to hide, but Max initially refuses to leave his family; he ultimately does so. Max's mother gives Max a piece of paper with Hans Hubermann's name and address.

Max hides in a storeroom for the next two years, and Walter periodically visits him with food; one day Walter tells Max that Max's family is gone. In 1939, Walter vists Hans, who agrees to keep his promise and help Max. Hans gives Walter some money, maps, directions, and a copy of *Mein Kampf* with a key, and in 1940 Max makes the dangerous journey to Molching.

THE WRATH OF ROSA

Rosa finds Max and Hans in the kitchen and gives Max some pea soup. Liesel silently watches them. Max vomits because his hunger has made him less able to hold down food.

LIESEL'S LECTURE

Max sleeps in a spare bed in Liesel's room. The next morning Liesel is kept home from school. In the basement, Hans tells Liesel about what happened to him in the war. Hans tells Liesel in no uncertain terms that she must never tell anyone about Max. Hans explains in detail what would happen if she did: Hans would burn Liesel's books, Liesel would be taken away, and Hans, Rosa, and Max would all be taken away and never return. Liesel cries uncontrollably.

THE SLEEPER

Max sleeps for three days, and Liesel watches him with fascination. When Max awakes, Liesel is staring at him.

THE SWAPPING OF NIGHTMARES

Summary and Analysis of Part Four

Max resolves to sleep in the cold basement from now on, hidden by a drop sheet and some paint cans. Max feels guilty and ashamed to go on hiding. After a few days, Liesel is made to take dinner down to Max. She sees Max reading *Mein Kampf* and tries to ask if it is a good book, but fails.

In the weeks that follow, Rosa's acts very subdued. She loses another laundry customer, but does not yell about it. Rudy and Liesel walk to school as usual, and Rudy first mentions a sadistic Hitler Youth leader named Franz Deutscher. Liesel still visits Ilsa Hermann and becomes fascinated by a book called *The Whistler*. Meanwhile Max's health deteriorates in the cold basement.

In early December, Hans brings Liesel to the basement to resume their lessons and finds Max frozen and sickly. Max begins sleeping on the floor by the fire in Hans and Rosa's bedroom. At Christmas, Hans Junior does not come home, but Trudy does. Trudy is not told about Max. Max apologizes for Hans' son not coming home, and Hans says that his son has the right to be stubborn.

Max overhears Liesel remark that his hair looks like feathers. By the fire, Liesel finally asks Max whether *Mein Kampf* is a good book, and Max says that it is saved his life. Max begins telling the story of his life over the next few weeks. Hans remarks that Liesel, too, enjoys fighting, and Liesel is surprised that he knows about the time she beat up Ludwig Schmeikl.

Max and Liesel both have nightmares, and one night Liesel asks Max about them. Max tells her he sees himself waving goodbye to his family, and Liesel tells him about her brother. Liesel brings Max a newspaper she finds in a garbage can, and Max gratefully does the crossword. On Liesel's birthday, Hans and Rosa give her *The Mud Men*, a book about a "strange father and son," and Max apologizes for not getting her anything. Liesel graciously hugs Max for the first time, and Max wonders what he could do for her.

PAGES FROM THE BASEMENT

Max cuts out pages from *Mein Kampf* and paints them white. He draws on them a story called *The Standover Man*, which he gives to Liesel. Liesel reads it three times then goes down to the basement and sleeps beside Max.

Analysis

The question of whether or not Hans is a coward is solved in this part. Hans' life is miraculously saved by a Jew in World War I, and for the rest of his life Hans is gracious to Jews despite the threat of imprisonment in a concentration camp for helping them in the wake of *Kristallnacht* -- indeed, Hans is lucky that he is not taken away for vandalizing a Nazi Party office. Risking his life to hide Max is Hans' courageous payback for Max's father Erik's good deed. Hans feels guilty over the fact that Erik, who had a son, died while childless Hans survived. By caring for Max, who still suffers from the loss of his father at a young age, Hans performs an important fatherly duty.

Max's fighting streak and defiant attitude contrast with the sickly, hiding person he has become in the Hubermanmn's basement. Max, who has resolved not to die without a fight, feels deep shame for the fact that he survives while his family has likely died. Yet Max's very existence and will to survive represents defiance against Hitler's racial extermination policies. Hans cleverly subverts Nazism by using a copy of Hitler's book *Mein Kampf* -- the very wellspring of Nazi ideology -- to assist in hiding a Jew. Max briefly considers giving the book, his only possession, to Liesel for her birthday, but likens that to a lamb handing a knife to a butcher. Instead Max also subverts Nazism by physically whitewashing the pages of *Mein Kampf* and painting an entirely different story over them. The text of *Mein Kampf*, riveted with attacks on the Jewish race, peeks through under a story about the friendship between a hidden Jew and a German girl.

The Standover Man is one of two complete illustrated stories that appear within *The Book Thief*. The story is of a bird who is scared of men standing over him: the plot is identical to Max's own life. The first "standover man" is his father, who vanishes at a young age. As a boy, he enjoys fighting, and whenever he loses another boy would be standing over him. When he comes to a safe house, it is a girl, not a man, standing over him. They share interests ("TRAIN," "DREAMS," "FISTS"), and the girl says he looks like something else. The picture on this page is of a man looking into a mirror and seeing a bird -- this is a reference to Liesel's comment that Max's hair looks like feathers. The girl asks the bird about his dreams, and both his and Liesel's recurring nightmares are pictured: Max saying goodbye to his family, and Liesel sleeping with her younger brother at the side of her bed. The bird now thinks they are friends, and that on her birthday the girl gave a gift to him, a hug. The "best standover man" he has ever known is not a man, but a girl. The final page is Liesel reading in the basement, with words like "VALUABLE" and "DAYLIGHT" written on the wall: this is a reference to Liesel's basement writing practice.

The idea of Max being represented by a bird suggests that while he is physically "caged" in the basement, his spirit is free and proves indomitable by the Nazis. The "standover men" in Max's life suggest his inner vulnerability: losing his father at a young age, for example, is compared with losing a fight. Yet a girl, not a man, standing over him brings him comfort as they become friends. Max has reached perhaps the most vulnerable point of his life thus far: he can continue to survive only at the mercy of the Hubermanns. His friendship with Liesel brings him such comfort that his best standover man is a young figure of compassion, not antagonism, and loyalty, not abandonment.

Abandonment is a key element of the lives of both Max and Liesel. They each have nightmares: one where Liesel is "abandoned" by her mother and brother, another where Max "abandons" his family. Neither of these episodes should be called true, deliberate abandonment, but both characters obviously feel guilty and deeply saddened by them. Significantly, Germany and her passion for war and violence is the central cause to the novel's abandonment episodes. Max's father dies in the first German war, and Hans' son has abandoned his father to fight in the second. Likewise, Hitler's persecution of Jews and Communists has divorced Max and Liesel from their old families.

Summary and Analysis of Part Five

Summary

THE FLOATING BOOK (Part I)

This section foreshadows events that happen later in the book. Rudy is standing in icy water, holding a soggy book and asking Liesel for a kiss. Death admits that Liesel will die and says he would have liked to have witnessed Liesel kissing his dead body.

THE GAMBLERS (A SEVEN-SIDED DIE)

A series of events over the course of 1941 are described, each compared with the roll of a die. In April, Max asks Liesel to cut his hair. In early May, Liesel continues to read *The Whistler* at Ilsa's home, and imagines herself confiding in Ilsa about Max. As Liesel prepares to go, Ilsa offers the book to her, but she refuses. On her way home, Liesel finds a newspaper for Max. Max and Liesel spend time reading together in the basement. In mid-May, Liesel's soccer team trounces Rudy's, and she excitedly tells Max. Max asks her to descibe the sky, and he draws her description on the wall, with the two of them walking on a cloud.

At the end of May, Max begins exercising again through a series of push-ups. He fantasizes about fighting Adolf Hitler in a boxing ring. The crowd -- millions of Germans -- cheers for Hitler and abuses Max, who arrives alone. Even the referee is biased towards Hitler. There is only one round, and Hitler punches Max for hours. Max falls, but slowly rises before the count, then at last aims a series of blows at Hitler's mustache. Hitler falls, then returns to his feet, removes his gloves, and addresses the crowd. Hitler delivers a speech threatening that Max is plotting against them, trying to enslave them. He asks them to come into the ring to "defeat this enemy together," and they do. In the end, a girl comes in with a newspaper and tells Max that the crossword is empty, then the fantasy is over. A few nights later Max tells Liesel about his recurring dream of fighting Hitler and that he is training for it. In early June, Max, Liesel, Hans and Rosa remove and paint over the pages of *Mein Kampf* then replace them in preparation for a new book.

Germany invades the Soviet Union in late June, and Rosa loses her last customer: the mayor and his wife Ilsa, who have to cut back while they advise others to prepare for harder times ahead. On Liesel's last visit, Ilsa begs her to take *The Whistler*, which she does at first. But Liesel feels so angry that she returns and yells at Ilsa, attacking her for being wealthy and arrogant and telling her to face the fact that her son is dead. Liesel throws the book on the ground and sees Ilsa as having been beaten up by her words. Back at home, Liesel tells Rosa that she called the mayor's wife pathetic, and that is why Ilsa fired them. Rosa does not think Liesel is capable of insulting Ilsa for obsession over her dead son, and calmly accepts the news of having been fired.

RUDY'S YOUTH

Rudy is having trouble with the Hitler Youth leader, an older boy named Franz Deutscher. When Rudy sticks up for Tommy Mueller, who has developed hearing problems and has trouble marching, the two are forced to perform a series of drills in the mud. Rudy tells Liesel what happened and tries to compel her to kiss him, but she doesn't.

THE LOSERS

Rudy and Liesel return to the group of young thieves and meet their new leader: Viktor Chemmel, a wealthy boy who steals for enjoyment. Liesel considers the new leader a cruel tyrant, in contrast to the last leader Arthur Berg. After they steal, Viktor gives Rudy and Liesel just one apple. When Rudy complains, Viktor beats him. Rudy spits on Viktor's feet, and Viktor vows to make Rudy pay for it at a later date.

SKETCHES

Max begins drawing sketches in the newly-blank pages of *Mein Kampf*. One cartoon shows Hitler singing before a saluting crowd with the caption "Not the Fuhrer - the conductor!" Another shows a couple standing atop a moutnain of dead bodies looking at a swastika Sun; one says, "Isn't it a lovely day..." Curious, Liesel sees these two pages and is deeply frightened by them.

THE WHISTLER AND THE SHOES

Rudy leaves a Hitler Youth meeting covered in manure, blaming Franz Deutscher. Rudy and Liesel agree to steal something as a way of giving Rudy a victory. Liesel brings Rudy to the mayor's house with the intention of stealing *The Whistler*, though Rudy things they are trying to get food. Liesel climbs through an open window and gets the book; they race off at first but Rudy loses her shoes and has to go back and retrieve them. When they get to their homes, Rudy for the first time calls Liesel "book thief."

THREE ACTS OF STUPIDITY BY RUDY STEINER

Rudy foolishly steals a large potato from Thomas Mamer's grocery in full view of many people. Mamer is about to call the police when Rudy spots one of his teachers and begs him to explain how poor Rudy is. The teacher does so convincingly, and Rudy is let go.

At a Hitler Youth meeting, Rudy is asked by his Hitler Youth leader Franz Deutscher when Hitler's birthday is; Rudy responds with Christ's birthday and is punished. Sometime later, Rudy sees Deutscher on the street and throws a rock at him. In front of Tommy, Liesel, and Rudy's younger sister Kristina, Deutscher savagely beats

Rudy. When Rudy is on the ground, Deutscher pulls out a knife and asks again about Hitler's birthday. Rudy replies, "Easter Monday," and Deutscher cuts Rudy's hair.

A few weeks later Rudy and Tommy begin skipping Hitler Youth meetings. Ultimately, they joined the Flieger Division, a youth group for aviation that mostly built model airplanes.

THE FLOATING BOOK (Part II)

Rudy and Liesel see Franz Deutscher on the street and avoid him, but run into Viktor Chemmel. Viktor takes Liesel's book *The Whistler* and throws it into the freezing Amper River. Rudy jumps in and retrieves it. Rudy lingers waist-deep in the cold water and asks Liesel for a kiss for the last time.

Analysis

The power of words to impel violence is explored in this part. Liesel's tirade against Ilsa is perhaps her cruellest moment since beating Ludwig Schmeikl. Liesel tells Ilsa, who has suffered for years over the death of her son, to get over it and pictures Ilsa's face as bloodied and battered from this verbal abuse. Liesel is genuinely angered about Ilsa firing Rosa, and does not regret what she said, though she later tells Hans that she is going to hell.

In Max's fantasies of fighting Hitler, he can take hours of punches one-on-one, then beat the Fuhrer in just seven blows. Yet Hitler then announces that Max is a threat to the German people and commands them to defeat him. Max's cartoon depicting Hitler as a conductor illustrates Hitler's total control over the German people, who obey his commands no matter how violent or illogical they are. Max sees himself as up against an entire brainwashed nation, yet he maintains his fortitude as he exercises.

Just as Arthur Berg from Part Three was one half of a Communist allegory, Viktor Chemmel represents the other, darker half. Chemmel is wealthy, selfish, arbitrary, and cruel for the sake of cruelty. Chemmel perhaps represents the violent excesses of Stalinism, though can also serve as a Hitler stand-in. He steals merely for fun and quotes Hitler's rhetoric: "We must take what is rightfully ours!" Liesel notes how after Arthur Berg left the gang of thieves, none of the other boys took his place as leader -- they were followers, and Chemmel enjoyed telling people what to do. The other boys' blind obedience to Chemmel, even when it is clear that Chemmel does not act in their best interests and is a less effective leader than Berg, is disturbingly similar to the Nazis' obedience to Hitler.

Rudy proves himself to be gallant, foolish, and quite rebellious in this part. Merely by refusing to tell Franz Deutscher Hitler's birthday, Rudy brings upon himself merciless physical punishment -- such is the price of defiant words. The same goes for Rudy's willingness to talk back to Chemmel. Rudy's "losses" here are compensated by his rescue of Liesel's book from the freezing river and the fact that he stands waist-deep in "devastatingly cold water" for a minute. Rudy's apparent selflessness comes with the hidden agenda of wanting a kiss from Liesel, yet by exhibiting such tolerance for physical abuse, Rudy convincingly "proves" his love for Liesel.

Summary and Analysis of Part Six

Summary

DEATH'S DIARY: 1942

Death dryly comments on some of the devastation of World War II, such as the Jews incinerated in Nazi extermination camps and the poorly-armed Russian soldiers being slaughtered by the hundreds of thousands on the Eastern Front. Death likens war to a demanding boss.

THE SNOWMAN

In late 1941, Liesel is 13. On Christmas, she brings pots of snow down to the basement for Max, and they build a snowman, lifting Max's spirits greatly. Soon after, though, Max's health deteriorates, and in mid-February 1942, he collapses, unconscious. He is placed in Liesel's room.

THIRTEEN PRESENTS

Five days later, Max awakes very briefly. Death remarks that it actually visited the room when Liesel was absent and prepared to take Max's soul, but felt a struggle and withdrew. A week later, Max briefly awakes again. Hans suggests that Liesel read to Max, so Liesel starts reading him *The Whistler*.

While playing soccer, the ball is run over by a car, and Liesel takes it to Max as a gift. She brings Max further presents: a pinecone, a toy soldier, newspapers, etc. At one point Liesel sees a giant cloud and Hans suggests that she give it to Max by writing down a description of it. Liesel finishes *The Whistler*, but Max remains comatose.

FRESH AIR, AN OLD NIGHTMARE, AND WHAT TO DO WITH A JEWISH CORPSE

Liesel and Rudy decide to steal from the mayor's house again. Liesel sneaks in and takes a red book called *The Dream Carrier*. Death hints that Ilsa keeps her library window open so that Liesel can steal books. At home, Liesel starts reading the book to Max.

In mid-March Liesel overhears Hans and Rosa discussing what to do with Max's corpse should he die. Liesel insists that Max is not dead yet. That night Liesel has a nightmare about her brother, except this time she sees Max's face on her brother's body.

Eight days later Rosa enters Liesel's classroom and yells at her, then whispers to her that Max is awake. Rosa gives her the toy soldier, which Max said was his favorite. That afternoon Liesel sees Max awake with the soccer ball on his lap. Max is happy about the gifts, and Liesel continues reading to him in his convalescence.

DEATH'S DIARY: COLOGNE

On May 30, 500 people die in the first major bombing raid against a Germany city. Death says the sky was yellow, "like burning newspaper." A group of young children see empty fuel canisters floating down and collect them.

THE VISITOR

Nazi Party members go door to door inspecting basements to identify possible air raid shelter locations. Liesel, who is out on the street playing soccer, sees them and wonders how to go home and tell Hans without seeming suspicious. Liesel accidentally collides with another boy, and Rudy runs to get Hans, who carries Liesel home. Before Hans and Rosa have a chance to figure out how to hide Max, who has since been hidden again in the basement, the party members arrive. They inspect the basement alone, find nothing, and leave. Hans, Rosa, and Liesel go downstairs and find Max hiding behind the drop sheets holding a pair of rusty scissors. He apologizes.

THE SCHMUNZELER

Rudy knocks on the door and asks to see Liesel to check up on her. He teases her for being a thief and smelling like cigarettes, and she shuts the door on him.

DEATH'S DIARY: THE PARISIANS

Death describes the desperation of those trapped inside gas chambers. Death says that it invokes the name of God whenever it tries to understand the gas chambers. God never says anything. Death describes its desolation on June 23, 1942, the first day of operation at the gas gambers in Auschwitz.

Analysis

Death frames Part Six with three sections of dark commentary about the growing devastation of World War II. The bombing of Cologne, a major German city, and the blood-soaked Eastern Front against the USSR indicate Nazi Germany's steadily weakening position. Along with the introduction of gas chambers at the Auschwitz concentration camp, these historical events foreshadow the devastation soon to reach the fictional town of Molching. When the Nazis inspect the Hubermanns' basement for a possible bomb shelter location, the fear that they will discover a hidden Jew overshadows the important indication that Allied bombing raids have become a real threat all across the German heartland.

Liesel's small acts of kindness and devotion towards Max illustrate the loving bond that has developed between the two. Max has in a way morphed into a surrogate for Liesel's dead brother, and Liesel's desperate fight to keep Max alive is one indication of the development of her character: Liesel is four years older now, and while she has not yet hit puberty, she has noticeably matured both intellectually and emotionally.

The Hubermanns' noble desperation to keep Max alive and hidden from the Nazis is a remarkable contrast to the horrors taking place in Germany's death camps. Death's description of the gas chamber is particularly wretching, and the consummately cynical narrator seems to break down emotionally. Notably, Death says the name of God while thinking about the Holocaust. The metaphysics and theology of Death (the character) and dying are not explained in the novel. Death's relationship to God -- or to any other spiritual being, for that matter -- is also ambiguous. To Death, "God never says anything," and to where Death delivers human souls is not explained. As Death carries away the souls from Auschwitz, it again tries to distract itself with colors: the sky turns from "silver to gray to the color of rain," and Death imagines the sky past that, "knowing without question that the sun was blond, and the endless atmosphere was a giant blue eye." The notion that God was "absent" during the death of six million Jews -- God's "chosen people" -- is an enduring theological controversy. Death's frustration in receiving no response or comfort from God echoes this idea, and the "giant blue eye" hidden by the dark clouds over Auschwitz is symbolic of God.

Summary and Analysis of Part Seven

Summary

CHAMPAGNE AND ACCORDIONS

In summer 1942, Molching, a small town outside Munich, prepares for bombing raids. Hans finds extra painting work due to the need to paint windows and blinds black. Liesel goes out with him and is impressed by Hans' cleverness and talent as a painter. One afternoon, Hans accepts some champagne in lieu of payment and gives Liesel a glass. Death writes that at this time, Liesel is the happiest she will ever be.

THE TRILOGY

Rudy spends the summer training for the upcoming Hitler Youth carnival, in which he intends to win four track competitions and show up Franz Deutscher, the Hitler Youth leader. Rudy wins the first three events but is disqualified from the fourth for two false starts. Later, Rudy tells Liesel that he disqualified himself on purpose and leaves his gold medals with her.

Liesel steals another novel from the mayor's home: a green book titled *A Song in the Dark*. She does so alone and without Rudy. A week later, Rudy brings Liesel to the mayor's home and points out a book that has seemingly been placed intentionally on a closed window. Liesel steals the book, *The Complete Duden Dictionary and Thesaurus*. As the two leave on bikes, Liesel turns around and sees the mayor's wife Ilsa Hermann standing in the window motionlessly waving to her. Inside the book is a letter from Ilsa to Liesel, in which Ilsa reveals she has known about the book stealing and is amused by it; she invites Liesel to come in through the front door instead of breaking in. Liesel returns to the mayor's house and tries to knock on the door but apparently cannot bring herself to do so.

ThE SOUND OF SIRENS

Hans has purchased a radio, which will broadcast air raids with a *cuckoo* sound before the sirens start. One night there is an air raid, and Rosa, Hans, and Liesel leave for a bomb shelter down the road. Max remains alone in the Hubermanns' basement, which has been deemed too shallow to be a shelter. On the street, everyone carries their most precious possessions -- Liesel takes her books.

The shelter is in the basement of the Fielders; 22 people are there, including the Steiners, Frau Holtzapfel, and Pfiffikus. Everyone is deeply fearful; some are stoic, others more obviously apprehensive. Death wonders if these people deserved any better, how many had actively participated in Hitler's persecution of others, whether the children or those who were hiding Jews deserved to die. Death pities them, but less so than it pities the Holocaust victims -- Death remarks that the basements were survivable, but the gas chambers were not.

The raid ends, and everyone returns home. Max tells the Hubermanns that during the raid he went upstairs and looked out the window for a few seconds, the first time he had seen the outside world in nearly two years. He tells them the stars burned his eyes.

THE SKY STEALER

The first raid had been a false alarm. A real raid takes place on September 19. The young children in the basement cry. Liesel begins reading *The Whistler* out loud, and everyone else quietly listens. After the raid ends, they linger as Liesel reads the final two paragraphs of the chapter. Outside, Himmel Street is untouched but there is a cloud of dust in the air. Hans wonders if he should go out and help with recovery, but Rosa tells him to stay. Liesel tells Max about her reading in the shelter.

FRAU HOLTZAPFEL'S OFFER

Frau Holtzapfel, the neighbor who hates Rosa, offers her coffee ration and to stop spitting on the Hubermanns' door in exchange for Liesel coming to her home and reading her *The Whistler* twice a week. Death explains that Holtzapfel has two sons in Russia and that she is both "proud and afraid."

THE LONG WALK TO DACHAU

A convoy of trucks transporting Jews to the concentration camp at Dachau stops outside Molching. Death removes a soul from one of the trucks. The soldiers sadistically decide to "parade" the Jews through town. Liesel and Rudy are playing soccer on the street when they see the procession; Hans meets them with his paint cart and tries to persuade Liesel to leave, but Liesel is determined to stay.

All wearing yellow stars, the Jews are malnourished and in miserable condition. An older man keeps falling down then struggling to his feet to keep up. Out of the crowd of abusive Germans, Hans offers the man a piece of bread, and the man falls between Hans' feet crying and thanking him. The soldiers whip the Jew six times then whip Hans four times. Death remarks that the older Jew "would die like a human," but wonders "if that's such a good thing." Three other Jews fight over the piece of bread.

Some of the Germans abuse Hans and turn over his paint cart, but others silently help him to safety. Hans panics, worried that the Nazis would come to his house and find Max.

PEACE

That night Max departs the Hubermanns' home, leaving behind a gift to be given to Liesel when she is "ready." It has been arranged that Max and Hans would meet in the forest in four days; Hans only finds a note reading "You've done enough."

THE IDIOT AND THE COAT MEN

Later that night Hans anxiously awaits the Gestapo, and Liesel prays for Max's safety. The next morning, Hans wonders why nobody has come and worries that Max was sent out for no reason. Hans castigates himself for giving the older Jew a piece of bread, but Liesel tries to reassure him that he has done nothing wrong. Three weeks later Liesel sees two men in black coats on the street and tells Hans the Gestapo is here. Hans runs out and yells that he is the one they want; they tell him that he is "a little old for our purposes" and instead go to the Steiners' home seeking Rudy.

Analysis

The image of Jewish prisoners en route to a concentration camp being "paraded" through Molching is a dark simulacrum of the Hitler Youth carnival, another Nazi civic event. The swift athletics of Rudy and the other runners contrasts with the shambling motions of the emaciated Jews. Both events are presided over by ambitious young followers of Hitler. Rudy appears to succeed in showing up Franz Deutscher, the cruel Hitler Youth leader, and he appears to do it on his own terms, willingly disqualifying himself from the final race. By contrast, the Jews are entirely at the will of the Nazi soldiers, some of whom only boys. Yet Rudy is also condemned, as the two agents who visit his home intend to recruit him for the military, in no small part because of his athletic accomplishments at the carnival.

Hans appears to have given the bread to the older Jew almost instinctively, without thought. Liesel is deeply impressed by Hans' brave and selfless humanity, yet Hans regrets his action. Hans has brought increased scrutiny towards his family, and Max can no longer safely remain with the Hubermanns. In offering a piece of bread to a frail Jew who is virtually certain to die, Hans endangers the life of the healthier, younger, and freer Max. Moreover, the older Jew, who does not even take the bread, is harshly punished. By this line of reasoning, Hans made an illogical and foolish decision that harmed many people without helping anyone. Yet, the moral dimensions of Hans' tiny act of kindness must be considered in light of the political atmosphere of Nazi Germany. Nazi ideology considered the Jews to be subhuman; by breaking from the abusive crowd and publicly offering the elderly Jew a bit of food, Hans treats the man as a human being. Not everyone in the crowd condemns Hans afterwards; some silently help him, perhaps because they too are horrified by the Nazis' inhumanity. While apparently ineffectual or even counterproductive, Hans' brave deed is his willingness to go up against the Nazis at a time when every other German, even those who were against the Nazis or sympathetic towards the Jews, quietly followed Hitler. Before the war, when Hans painted Jewish homes and refused to join the Nazi party, his actions alone could not stop either the deportation of the Jews or the war. Yet Hans was courageous then for his willingness to defy the Nazis, and Hans' defiance in this part of the novel is comparable to that episode.

Ilsa's "gift" of the *Duden Dictionary* and implicit forgiveness of Liesel for Liesel's outburst of rage shows the complexity of Ilsa's emotions. Quiet and still brooding over the death of her son in 1918, Ilsa says more in her letter to Liesel than she has spoken over the course of the book. Prior to this part, Ilsa appeared distant, and her intentions in inviting Liesel to read in her library were ambiguous. The letter makes clear that Ilsa cares about Liesel and wants to see her continue to read and learn. Ilsa might see a part of her younger self in Liesel's precocity and daring. Ilsa shows through her letter that she too is clever and well-read; in not reporting Liesel to the authorities for stealing a banned book from the book burning, Ilsa also defies the law and becomes Liesel's accomplice. The adult Ilsa's continued mourning over the death of her son might impel her to want Liesel to recover from the death of her brother. Although it is unclear how much Ilsa knows about Liesel's history, Liesel notably sees an apparation of her brother when she tries to knock on Ilsa's door to thank her for the dictionary.

For Liesel and her reading, Ilsa is an encouraging figure. When Liesel calms everyone in the bomb shelter by reading *The Whistler*, she begins to realize the power of words to affect human emotions. Even the feud between Frau Holtzapfel and Rosa subsides when Liesel begins reading to the former.

Summary and Analysis of Part Seven

Summary and Analysis of Part Eight

Summary

DOMINOES AND DARKNESS

In the Steiner household, Rudy and the younger children are setting up dominoes while their parents argue with the two Nazi agents in the kitchen about inducting Rudy into a special military school. Rudy eavesdrops on the conversation as the children set off the dominoes by candlelight. Rudy understands that by winning three gold medals at the Hitler Youth carnival, he proved himself not only to his former tormentor Franz Deutscher but to everyone. Rudy's parents refuse to let him go.

THE THOUGHT OF RUDY NAKED

Earlier, a nurse and a doctor have Rudy and two other boys remove their clothes for a physical examination at school. The nurse explains to a teacher in the room that they are creating a "new class of physically and mentally advanced Germans." The doctor says he will take two of them.

A day after the Nazis visited the Steiner household, Rudy tells Liesel about these two events. For days afterward, Liesel has visions of Rudy in the nude.

PUNISHMENT

After the departure of Max, Hans has lost his optimism. He no longer plays the accordion and eagerly awaits his punishment for helping the elderly Jew on the street. In early November, Hans' application to join the Nazi Party is approved, several years after submission. Two days later, Hans is drafted into the German army, which is desperate for new recruits following severe losses against the Soviet Union. Rudy's father Alex Steiner is also drafted.

THE PROMISE KEEPER'S WIFE

The night before Hans is to leave for training, Hans and Alex get drunk at the Knoller against the wishes of their wives. The next morning, Rosa rouses Hans with a bucket of cold water. Liesel unsuccessfully begs Hans not to leave, and Hans asks her to look after his accordion and to continue reading if there is another raid. Rudy and Liesel are devastated by their losses; Rudy tries to get Liesel to run away with him to find and kill Hitler. Liesel reflects on all the people she has lost: her mother, her brother, Max, and now Hans. On their way home, they walk past Alex Steiner's tailor shop, which is now closed.

That night, Liesel awakens and finds Rosa in the living room sitting on the edge of her bed with Hans' accordion.

THE COLLECTOR

Alex is sent to an army hospital in Vienna, where he is tasked with mending clothes. Hans is sent to Essen, where he is given an undesirable job with the Air Raid Special Unit: his unit must stay above ground during air raids to put out fires, prop up buildings, and save people. Everyone in the unit had done something impolitic to get this assignment. Hans tells them about his having given bread to a Jew; the Sergeant laughs and tells him he is lucky to be alive.

The job is smoky and incredibly dangerous. Occasionally people would roam through the haze and rubble seeking a missing loved one. In one shift, a bleeding old man asks Hans for help; Hans carries him to safety then finds the man is dead. Later, Hans trips over the corpse of a young boy while rushing from a building; a woman comes down the street asking if anyone has seen her son Rudolf, and the sergeant is unable to bring himself to tell her about the dead boy. The name makes Hans think about Rudy Steiner.

THE BREAD EATERS

Back in Molching, Liesel spends the rest of 1942 thinking about three men, Hans, Max, and Alex. She continues reading *The Whistler* to Frau Holtzapfel. In the fall, another parade of Jews takes place, and Liesel rushes to see if Max is among them. In the middle of December, a third, smaller collection of Jews is marched down the street. Rudy shows Liesel a bag containing six pieces of bread. They place the bread on the street in advance of the Jews and hide; Liesel hears Rudy's stomach growl. When the procession arrives, Jews snatch up the bread. A soldier notices Liesel and Rudy, and the two run. Liesel is kicked in the backside by a soldier, but the two receive no other punishment. Max is not among this group either.

THE HIDDEN SKETCHBOOK

Another air raid takes place shortly before Christmas, and Liesel again reads to the shelter.

After the raid, Rosa gives Liesel the present Max made for her: a book called *The Word Shaker*. The book contains pages full of sketches and stories. On page 117 is a lightly-illustrated story, a fable about "The Word Shaker":

A man, apparently Hitler, decideds he would rule the world. One day he sees a mother scolding her child until he cries then minutes later speaking very softly to him until he smiles. The Fuhrer decides he will rule the world with words. He plants the seeds of words and symbols across his country and cultivates them. He beckons people with his freshly-picked words and places them on a conveyor belt, through which they are hypnotized with words and outfitted with symbols. The demand for his words becomes so great that people are hired to cultivate the massive forests of words; some, called "word shakers," are employed to climb the trees and throw the words to people below.

A small, skinny girl is the "best word shaker of her region because she knew how powerless a person could be" without words. She could climb higher than anyone else. The girl befriends a man who is despised by her homeland; when he is sick, she sheds a tear on his face. The tear, made of friendship, becomes a seed, which the girl plants and cultivates. The tree steadily grows to the tallest in the forest. The Fuhrer, enraged, orders the tree cut down and takes an axe to it. The girl defiantly climbs to the top of it, and the Fuhrer's ax is unable to make a dent in the tree trunk. For months, the girl remains in the tree, and the Fuhrer's soldiers are unable to destroy it as long as she is there.

A new axman arrives, but instead of an ax, he takes a hammer and places nails up the tree. Using the nails as footholds, he climbs up to the girl, miles high above the clouds. The man turns out to be the girl's friend from earlier. They climb down together, and the massive tree falls, crushing part of the forest and creating a new path through it. They walk down the horizontal trunk; behind them, most of the onlookers had returned to the rest of the forest, but the two friends can hear "voices and words behind them, on the word shaker's tree."

THE ANARCHIST'S SUIT COLLECTION

On Christmas Eve, Liesel and Rudy go to his father's store, where she gets him a "present": a navy blue suit.

Analysis

"The Word Shaker" is the second of two stories given by Max to Liesel and reproduced in the novel. It is a simple allegory for Nazi Germany and the power of words and compassion. Hitler's rhetorical style is likened to a mother who scolds her son, damaging his feelings, then speaks to softly to him, perking him up. He decides he can control people through words and conquer the world without having to fire a gun. He grows a forest of propaganda, hypnotizes people with his words, and hires them to maintain the forest and propagandize for him. The girl, who represents Liesel, knows the power of words as well as Hitler. She starts off as a word shaker, but her love for her persecuted friend causes her to plant an impenetrable tree that grows miles high, much higher than any of Hitler's trees. Only when her friend arrives does she finally climb down, allowing the tree to fall and destroy a chunk of Hitler's forest. Although the tree does not destroy the entire forest, it carves a new path through it, and others follow the man and girl as they walk together down the horizontal trunk.

Liesel's great compassion towards Max and defiance of the Nazis are symbolized by the massive tree that Hitler cannot cut down. Even though the tree does not destroy all of Hitler's forest, it destroys enough of it to create a path that other resisters to Hitler's propaganda can follow. Thus a singular act of defiance reverberates throughout the country and inspires others to defy Hitler as well. The immense height of the girl's tree suggests that her friendship is so boundless and so inspired that it is more powerful than Hitler's propaganda of hatred. Thus can words of sincere love effectively combat words of self-serving cruelty.

Reading "The Word Shaker" effectively caps Liesel's realization of the awesome power of words. Throughout the novel, Hitler's propaganda pervades the lives of the principal characters and impels the entire nation to wage an horrific war and engage in genocide. There is a direct link from Hitler's book *Mein Kampf* to any number of tragedies that have affected Liesel's life: the deaths of her mother and brother, the persecution of Max, and the recent loss of Hans and Rudy's father to the war. "The Word Shaker" validates the use of words and defiance which spring from compassionate intentions to combat words which spring from hatred. Liesel herself touched on this lesson early on, when she beat up Ludwig Schmeikl for insulting her illiteracy; she later apologized after witnessing the book burning and the Nazi speaker's invective against Jews and Communists. Like the girl in "The Word shaker," Liesel, as well as her tall foster father Hans, is capable of maintaining a potent defiance against Nazi cruelty. Max's story insists that Liesel's compassion is strong enough to destroy miles of Hitler's evil.

Summary and Analysis of Part Nine

Summary

THE NEXT TEMPTATION

With Rudy, Liesel takes a plate of cookies and another book, *The Last Human Stranger*, from the mayor's house. She encounters Ilsa and realizes that the library is hers. Ilsa explains that the books are mostly hers; some belonged to her son. Liesel is touched by the idea that the woman owns a roomful of books. Liesel and Rudy eat half the cookies on the way home and share the rest with Tommy Muller.

THE CARDPLAYER

Meanwhile near Essen, Hans and the rest of his brigade are playing cards for cigarettes. A young man named Reinhold Zucker, who gloats when he wins, accuses Hans of cheating; by contrast, whenever Hans wins a hand he graciously gives his colleagues a cigarette back. Reinhold refuses this; he despises Hans.

THE SNOWS OF STALINGRAD

In January 1943, Liesel goes to Frau Holtzapfel's to read and encounters an old-looking man with a bloody, bandaged hand. He tells Liesel to come back later; three hours later, he visits Liesel's home. He is one of Holtzapfel's sons, Michael, and he has just returned from the Battle of Stalingrad. Liesel lights a cigarette for him. Michael informs Rosa that his brother died in a makeshift hospital; he also tells her that he heard Hans Junior is alive there.

Death explains how Michael's brother Robert died: on a freezing cold January day in Russia, Robert's legs were blown off. He was brought to the temporary hospital and died three days later, his brother at his side. At Frau Holtzapfel's home, Liesel reads to Michael and his crying mother.

THE AGELESS BROTHER

Liesel returns the empty plate to Ilsa Hermann's front door and imagines that her dead brother would be six years old forever. Rosa still sits with Hans' accordion and prays for the safe return of her husband and son.

THE ACCIDENT

On the truck carrying Hans' unit, Reinhold Zucker demands to switch seats with Hans; unwilling to argue, Hans complies. A tire blows out and the driver loses control of the truck. Zucker is the only one who dies in the accident, and Hans says that it should have been him. Instead, Hans' leg is injured, and his Sergeant says he will recommend Hans be given rest then sent to Munich for office work, a much safer assignment. He says to Hans, "You're lucky you're a good man, and generous with the cigarettes."

THE BITTER TASTE OF QUESTIONS

In February Liesel and Rosa receive a letter from Hans telling them that he is coming home. Barbara Steiner is ecstatic about the news, and Rudy appears happy, but internally wonders why Hans and not his father will be returning.

ONE TOOLBOX, ONE BLEEDER, ONE BEAR

Rudy, who has been steadily growing angrier since his father's recruitment, takes a metal toolbox up the street; the box contains burglary tools and a teddy bear. Liesel runs out to meet him. Rudy tells her that she is not a real thief since Ilsa practically lets her in; he says that stealing is "what the army does. Taking your father, and mine." Rudy plans on breaking into one of the wealthier residents' homes. He tells Liesel that the teddy bear is to calm down a kid should he encounter one. Ultimately, Rudy is unable to bring himself to steal. Later, he uses the toolbox to carry possessions for air raids.

In March there is another air raid. Frau Holtzapfel refuses to leave her home, and Michael and Rosa are uanble to get her out. Liesel tells her that if she doesn't come to the shelter, Liesel will stop coming to read to her and she will have lost her only friend; Frau Holtzapfel still refuses, so the others leave her for the Fiedlers' basement. Michael regrets leaving his mother, but Frau Holtzapfel arrives. The raid is long, and Liesel reads 54 pages to the group.

After the raid, Rudy's younger sister notices a small fire and smoke coming from near the river. Rudy, with his toolbox, heads there through the forest, and Liesel follows. There is a downed plane. Rudy takes the teddy bear from his toolbox and places it on the pilot. The pilot thanks him in English and dies. Death arrives to carry the man's soul away and recognizes Liesel; Death is convinced that Liesel recognized its presence as well. Death remarks that it has been Hitler's most loyal servant.

HOMECOMING

After his convalescence, Hans is given a week home before being sent to Munich to do paperwork. He tells Liesel and Rosa about all that has happened to him, including the death of Reinhold Zucker. All that night, he sits by Liesel's bed; she wakes several times to see if he is still there.

Analysis

The apparent capriciousness of war and death has emotionally wracked the residents of Molching. As the Sergeant notes, Hans survives by having the fortune to be a good gambler and a kind man. Reinhold Zucker dies through his irrational animosity towards Hans; Zucker demands Hans' seat, which Hans considers to be the worst seat in the truck, for no other reason than petty aggression. Hans politely obliges; as a result, Zucker dies in the crash, and Hans is injured and given a transfer to a light assignment. Hans thus cheats death once more in another war.

Rudy grows angrier over his father's conscription and the fact that chance has brought Liesel's father and not his home. He sees Hitler and the Army as having stolen the men, and as a result he plans a violent burglary against the wealthier members of his town. Yet Rudy is unable to commit anything more than petty theft. This is perhaps a reflection of Rudy's ultimate powerlessness in the face of the German war machine; he cannot fight them with violence. Contrast this with "The Word Shaker's" notion that words are ultimately more powerful than bullets (as words can impel people to fight) and propaganda can be successfully countered with words of compassion and friendship. Instead of using the toolbox's contents to commit crime, Rudy ends up giving a teddy bear from it to a dying Allied pilot, a participant in the bombing raid that had just confined his family to an air raid shelter for hours. In addition to this obvious antagonism, there is a language barrier: The pilot thanks Rudy in English, and Rudy asks in German what he said. Rudy's act of compassion to the man bombing his homeland is not a small one: pilots shot down over enemy territory are in danger of being tortured or even lynched by citizens or soldiers outraged over bombing raids. Here intrepid Rudy is the first to meet the pilot, before other citizens quietly arrive, and his action sets an example for them. Rudy has thus demonstrated an acute recognition of the irrationality of hatred and of the fact that the war has ensnared and killed unwilling participants from both sides of the conflict.

The death of one of Frau Holtzapfel's sons sends her into a state of near-catatonia; she barely seems to recognize that her other son has returned home alive. Learning of the state of the Holtzapfel's sons makes Rosa worry about her own son, another participant in the Russian bloodbath. Introduced as a fiery character at the outset of the novel, Rosa has been steadily worn down and now appears emotionally deadened over the uncertain fates of her husband and son.

Summary and Analysis of Part Ten and Epilogue

Summary

THE END OF THE WORLD (Part I)

Death describes the bombing of Himmel Street to take place at the end of this part. Everyone dies sleeping except for Liesel, who is awake in the Hubermann's basement at the time of the raid. A rescue crew finds her clutching a book and asks why she was in the basement, as the air raid sirens failed to go off in time.

THE NINETY-EIGHTH DAY

After a week at home, Hans begins his simple office assignment in Munich. Three months later in Molching, Jews are marched through town on their way to perform forced clean-up work. Liesel again watches to see if Max is among them; Death explains that Max soon will be. Michael Holtzapfel commits suicide due to his guilt over surviving where his brother died.

THE WAR MAKER

Michael Holtzapfel's funeral takes place in July. The Allies bomb Hamburg, killing 45,000. Death remarks that the Germans "were starting to pay in earnest," and that despite Germany's military setbacks, Hitler had not been slackening off "in terms of war-making" and the extermination of the Jews.

WAY OF THE WORDS

Another batch of Jews is marched through town on their way to Dachau. Max is among them, and Liesel recognizes him by the way he scans the crowd of Germans looking for her. Liesel runs into the procession and latches onto Max. He tells her that he was captured a few months ago, halfway to Stuttgart. Max warns Liesel to let go of him, but she continues to walk with him. A soldier drags her away and throws her off. Liesel gets up and returns to Max; she mentions "The Word Shaker" and "The Standover Man." He stops walking, as do the rest of the Jews. They embrace, and Max is whipped while Liesel is dragged away again. Liesel is whipped as well, and Rudy in the crowd calls out to her as Max is forced off. Rudy and Tommy Muller pull Liesel away. Liesel tries to go after the disappearing procession, but Rudy restrains her, and she fights him.

CONFESSIONS

Liesel sullenly waits for Hans at the train station. Hans and Rosa learn about what happened; Hans tries to play the accordion that evening but cannot. Liesel stays in bed for three days. On the fourth day, she walks with Rudy down the road toward Dachau. She explains everything about Max to him. She shows Rudy the drawing of him Max made. Rudy is surprised she told Max about him; inwardly Liesel wants Rudy to kiss her and realizes that she loves him. Rudy will die in one month.

ILSA HERMANN'S LITTLE BLACK BOOK

Liesel heads to Ilsa Hermann's home, thinking a visit might cheer her up. She enters through a window and begins reading a book on the floor of Ilsa's library. Liesel does not know or care whether Ilsa is home; she contemplates all the people she has seen die and pictures Hitler's words at the center of it. She does not want to hope for Max and Alex Steiner anymore, "because the world does not deserve them." She rips up the book she was reading and says out loud, "What good are the words?" "Without words, the Fuhrer was nothing." She calls out Ilsa's name, but gets no response. Liesel writes a letter to Ilsa, in which she apologizes for destroying a book and says she will never return to punish herself.

Three days later, Ilsa arrives at Liesel's home. Ilsa tells her that, based on the letter, she can write well and gives her a blank book of lined paper; she asks Liesel not to punish herself, as Ilsa did over the death of her son. Liesel invites Ilsa in for coffee and bread. That night, Liesel goes down to the basement and begins writing a story titled *The Book Thief*.

THE RIB-CAGE PLANES

Liesel writes eleven pages of the story of her life, starting with her brother's death. Every night, Liesel goes down to the basement to write. Ten nights later, Liesel is asleep in the basement and doesn't hear the air raid siren; Hans wakes her to go to the shelter. On October 2, Liesel has finished.

THE END OF THE WORLD (Part II)

Death describes the bombing of Himmel Street. The sirens are too late. The first bomb hits Tommy Muller's apartment block; he and his family are asleep. Frau Holtzapfel is sitting awake in her kitchen. Frau Diller is asleep; her shop is destroyed, and her framed photo of Hitler is smashed. The Steiners are all asleep, and Rudy is in a bed with one of his sisters; Death recognizes him as the boy who gave the pilot a teddy bear. Death observes Rudy's soul and sees him pretending to be Jesse Owens, retrieving a book from the icy river, and imagining a kiss from Liesel; he makes Death cry. At last, Death takes Hans and Rosa. Hans' soul sits up and meets Death, passively ready to go; Hans' soul whispers Liesel's name, knowing that she is in the basement.

Death travels to other streets, but returns to Himmel for a single man. Death notices the recovery crew laughing and curiously watches. The crew pulls Liesel out; she panics and runs down her destroyed street. The crew informs her that her town has been bombed, and she tells them that they must get Hans, Rosa, and Max. Still holding her book, Liesel collapses to the ground, and a man seats her. She sees a worker carrying Hans' broken accordion case and offers to take it. Liesel drops the accordion when she sees the corpses laid out on the street. She sees Frau Holtzapfel first, then Rudy. She begs Rudy to wake up, then kisses him on the lips.

Liesel then sees Rosa and Hans. Crying, she tells Rosa's body about the day she arrived on Himmel Street, how Rosa informed her about Max waking up, and that she knew Rosa would sit with Hans' accordion. Liesel asks a worker for the accordion, and she places it by Hans' body. She envisions Hans rise and play the accordion beautifully, a cigarette hanging from his lips. She says goodbye to him.

The Book Thief is thrown onto a garbage truck along with other rubble. Death climbs onto the truck and takes it.

EPILOGUE

DEATH AND LIESEL

Death is now writing in the present, "many years" after these events. Liesel died yesterday in Sydney, Australia. She lived to a "very old age." Like Hans', her soul sat up to meet Death. In her final visions, she saw "her three children, her grandchildren, her husband," and others in her life, including Hans and Rosa, her brother, and Rudy.

WOOD IN THE AFTERNOON

After Himmel Street is cleared, Ilsa Hermann and the mayor take Liesel into their home. Liesel, still covered in dust and detritus from the bombing, does not bathe for the four days leading to the day of the funerals. Two ceremonies are held for the Steiners: one immediately after burial, and one after the return of Alex Steiner. Alex regrets not letting Rudy go to the Army school, and wishes that it had been himself and not his son who died. Liesel tells him about kissing Rudy's corpse.

MAX

After the war was over, Alex resumes his tailor work. Liesel often accompanies him. In October 1945, Max returns.

THE HANDOVER MAN

After Liesel dies, Death walks down the street with her and shows her *The Book Thief*, which Death has kept all these years. Death says that it read Liesel's book many times. Liesel asks if Death could understand it; Death does not respond. Death wants to ask her how the human race can be "so ugly and so glorious," but does not. Instead Death tells her the "only truth" it "truly knows": "I am haunted by humans."

Analysis

Max Vandenberg, the once-hidden Jew, survives a concentration camp, yet all but one of the good Germans of Himmel Street perish. In the end, both the Germans who openly supported the Nazis and those who quietly defied them received the same punishment that Death wondered was appropriate for the citizens of a nation guilty of violent persecution.

After seeing Max being marched to Dachau, Liesel gives up all hope, insisting that the world does not deserve the likes of Max or Alex Steiner. Surrounded by Ilsa's books, Liesel comes to view words -- Hitler's words -- as the source of the Nazis' violence, and wonders what good are words at all. This understanding that persecution and violence flows from propaganda is the culmination of Liesel's experiences, one half the lesson imparted by "The Word Shaker." Ilsa's gift of a blank book catalyzes Liesel's understanding of the second half, in which words of hope become the antidote to words of misery: Death remarks, "there would be punishment and pain, and there would be happiness, too. That was writing." By fate, Liesel's life is saved by both this gift and this realization, as she remains in her basement feverishly writing her life story during the air raid.

Death has posed the story of Liesel's life as one of many extraordinary tales of humanity that Death keeps for distraction from its often tragic work. In the prologue, Death explains that it is not the dead, but the survivors that it cannot stand to look at. Michael Holtzapfel is one such survivor who could not stand the guilt associated with having survived while his brother died. Alex Steiner sincerely wishes that he, and not his son Rudy, had died. Liesel, the "perpetual survivor," has faced this guilt over her brother's death since the beginning of the novel. Before the raid, Liesel was able to turn her life's tragedies into a novel that would be read and reread by the personification of Death itself. After the raid took Rudy and her foster parents, Liesel was nevertheless able to lead a long and fruitful life. The stories of survivors like her are tragic to Death, and Death is remarkably impressed by Liesel's uniquely human capacity to live past such personal devastation.

Ultimately, *The Book Thief* is framed by Death's ongoing contemplation of humanity. Death finds it impossible to weigh the value of human beings, with some capable of great malice and criminality like Hitler and others capable of great strength and bravery like Liesel and Hans: "I wanted to ask her how the same thing could be so ugly and so glorious, and its words and stories so damning and brilliant." Thus is Death haunted by humans, just as humans are haunted by Death. A jaded metaphysical being so used to dying could only be fearful of -- and, at times, amazed by -- those who live.

Suggested Essay Questions

1. **Consider Zusak's use of foreshadowing. By revealing how characters die early on, or the outcomes to certain events, does Zusak make the novel less suspenseful or more?**

   A proper response should cite specific examples of foreshadowing and make some explanation of why the technique is used. This could be Death's rationale: "It's the machinations that wheel us there that aggravate, perplex, interest, and astound me" (243). An essay arguing that the novel is more suspenseful because of foreshadowing should involve Death's selective and incomplete revelation of facts and should compare instances of foreshadowing with the actual descriptions of the events being foreshadowed.

2. **Why do Max and Liesel become friends? What do they have in common?**

   Initially Max and Liesel are apprehensive around each other, but they discover that they have something important in common: both have recurring nightmares involving the last time they saw their families alive. Both are political refugees evading Nazi persecution: Max is a Jew, Liesel's parents were Communists. Their similar backgrounds make Max's initial gift of *The Standover Man* important, as Max ultimately helps Liesel realize the power of words to delight and to harm others.

3. **Hans manages to survive two World Wars, seemingly by luck. Is Hans merely a fortunate man, or does he have other qualities that help him survive?**

   The argument that Hans is indeed lucky should be bolstered by references to other instances of luck or fate saving characters' lives: that the Nazis fail to find Max when inspecting the Hubermanns' basement, that Hans does not formally withdraw his application to join the Nazi Party and is thus spared from being sent to a concentration camp. One quality that helps Hans is his amiability. His friend Erik Vandenberg saves him in World War I, while his willingness to give up his seat to an antagonistic young soldier saves him again in World War II.

4. **Evaluate the pros and cons of Hans giving bread to an elderly Jew condemned to a concentration camp. Were the consequences worth the benefits?**

   Hans' action results in him and the frail, moribund Jew being whipped. Max is forced to leave because Hans' basement is no longer safe for him, and Hans is ultimately conscripted into a physically dangerous position in the military. Yet Hans' public compassion towards the Jew gives the man the feeling of humanity in a nation that has dehumanized him. Hans also sets an example for other German citizens in the crowd, some of whom help him after he is attacked.

5. **Why does Rudy seem to love Liesel immediately after they meet, and why does Liesel not recognize that she loves him until years after?**

Rudy is introduced as "one of those audacious little bastards who actually fancied himself with the ladies," and he is an impetuous character. He has a strong sense of justice and compassion, and early on he decides to take care of Liesel, an anxious new girl. Liesel is initially annoyed by Rudy's requests for a kiss, but her feelings towards him begin to change after Rudy gallantly retrieves Liesel's book from the icy cold river. Liesel's fixation on Rudy's physical exam is a rare moment of eroticization in the novel, one which might coincide with Liesel reaching puberty. Two important scenes where Liesel becomes nervous and desirous of Rudy: when Liesel gives Rudy a navy blue suit from his father's store, and when Liesel tells Rudy about Max.

6. **When Liesel reads aloud to the others in the bomb shelter for the first time, a voice inside her says, "This is your accordion." What does that mean?**

Hans' puts his soul into his accordion playing, and the music he produces is joyful. Through reading, Liesel is also able to bring comfort to others. More importantly, Liesel learns towards the end of the novel the capacity for words to cause both pain and happiness. This scene is part of Liesel's realization that she, like Max, can soothe others through words of friendship.

7. **The mayor's wife Ilsa Hermann strives to help and encourage Liesel throughout the novel, even after Liesel verbally abuses her. Why does Ilsa seem to take such a liking to Liesel?**

Although Ilsa may not actually realize it at first, both she and Liesel have experienced great losses in their lives: i.e., Ilsa's son, and Liesel's brother. Ilsa is an educated woman with her own library, and she might see a part of herself in Liesel's precocity and love of reading. Ilsa has been tormented by her son's death for over two decades, and she urges Liesel at the end of the novel not to let sorrow consume her life.

8. **Compare and contrast the two stories Max writes for Liesel, "The Standover Man" and "The Word Shaker." Why does Max only want Liesel to have the latter "when she's ready?"**

Both stories reference Max's persecution and his friendship with Liesel. "The Standover Man" is a more heavily illustrated story that Max gives to Liesel as Liesel is still just starting to read. The story is an early affirmation of their friendship. By contrast, "The Word Shaker" contains more text, and the political message is more serious and explicit. Max thinks Liesel might be too old for the allegory, but nevertheless does not want to frighten her with his caustic depiction of Hitler hypnotizing her entire country.

9. **What is the significance of Hitler's book *Mein Kampf* within the novel? How do different characters use it?**

Liesel realizes that *Mein Kampf* and Hitler's propaganda are the source of her misery: the reason for her parents' deaths, the reason for the war, and the reason Max is sent to a concentration camp. Max has a more ironic view, dryly telling Liesel that it "saved his life," as Hans used the book to help Max reach Molching. Max later whitewashes the pages of the book and uses them to write stories for Liesel.

10. **Why does Death tell Liesel that it is "haunted" by humans?**

Death has witnessed humans commit both acts of great cruelty and acts of great compassion. Death is unable to judge humanity because it cannot understand how humans are capable of both. Death considers the fate of survivors to be more tragic than the fate of the dead, perhaps because of Death's obvious familiarity with dying and blase attitude towards it. It can be argued that Death itself represents just one extreme between life and death, and is thus unable to comprehend the human condition of the living.

Notes on the Holocaust and Dachau

Originally published in 1925, *Mein Kampf* is largely predicated on Hitler's allegation of the existence of a massive Jewish conspiracy against the German people. After Hitler assumed absolute power in 1933, the Nazis enacted a series of laws meant to segregate and otherwise dehumanize the Jews. *Kristallnacht*, known as the Night of Broken Glass, was an organized nationwide pogrom that took place in 1938. By this point, all German Jews -- even those who had fought for Germany in World War I -- had been stripped of their rights as citizens and formally excluded from German society.

Hitler maintained his intention of eliminating Jews from Germany and, later, Germany's conquered possessions. In the initial stages of this process, German Jews were terrorized into emigrating; those who remained were ultimately rounded up and forced into concentration camps and labor camps. Jews were joined by homosexuals, gypsies, dissidents, Communists, and Polish and Soviet prisoners of war. Many prisoners engaged in forced labor for German corporations and armament factories, thus contributing to the war effort of the nation that condemned them. The infamous gas chambers at Auschwitz began operation in 1942; from that point on, captured and deported Jews were primarily sent straight to extermination camps, complexes built for the express purpose of efficiently and regularly murdering large numbers of people.

In 1933, the first concentration camp was established at Dachau in southeast Germany, outside the large city of Munich. The longest running Nazi concentration camp in continual operation, Dachau was not an extermination camp per se, yet tens of thousands of Jews and other prisoners died there; countless more were transferred from Dachau to actual extermination camps. Dachau was liberated by the United States Army in 1945 just a few weeks before Germany's surrender.

About six million Jews died in the Holocaust. Millions more -- members of other groups targeted for extermination by the Nazis in Hitler's quest for racial purity and world conquest -- perished as well. Up to 10% of Germany's population, civilians and soldiers, are estimated to have perished in Hitler's war.

Author of ClassicNote and Sources

Justin T. Cass, author of ClassicNote. Completed on November 20, 2009, copyright held by GradeSaver.

Updated and revised Damien Chazelle November 30, 2009. Copyright held by GradeSaver.

Markus Zusak. The Book Thief. New York: Knopf, 2005.

"Markus Zusak : Home of The Book Thief and I Am the Messenger." 2009-09-17. <http://www.randomhouse.com/features/markuszusak/index.html>.

"Markus Zusak (1975-) Biography - Personal, Addresses, Career, Honors Awards, Writings, Sidelights." 2009-09-16. <http://biography.jrank.org/pages/389/Zusak-Markus-1975.html>.

"Frequently Asked Questions about Dachau." 2009-09-11. <http://www.scrapbookpages.com/DachauScrapbook/DachauFAQ.html>.

"World War II Casualties." 2009-10-07. <http://fathersforlife.org/hist/wwiicas.htm>.

"History of Dachau concentration camp." 2009-10-05. <http://www.scrapbookpages.com/DachauScrapbook/overview.html>.

Quiz 1

1. **What is the color of Hans's eyes?**
   A. Silver
   B. Blue
   C. Black
   D. Brown

2. **Which book does Liesel steal first?**
   A. The Duden Dictionary
   B. The Shoulder Shrug
   C. The Grave-Digger's Handbook
   D. The Whistler

3. **Which country did Germany invade in September 1939?**
   A. Poland
   B. United Kingdom
   C. Soviet Union
   D. France

4. **Which major German city was bombed first?**
   A. Berlin
   B. Munich
   C. Cologne
   D. Molching

5. **At which battle was Michael Holtzapfel injured?**
   A. Berlin
   B. Moscow
   C. Leningrad
   D. Stalingrad

6. **Which of these characters does NOT die during World War II?**
   A. Hans Hubermann
   B. Frau Diller
   C. Ilsa Hermann
   D. Rudy Steiner

7. **Whose basement do the Hubermanns use as a bomb shelter?**
    A. The Holtzapfels'
    B. The Fiedlers'
    C. The Hermanns'
    D. The Steiners'

8. **Which book does Max give to Liesel?**
    A. The Duden Dictionary
    B. The Standover Man
    C. The Shoulder Shrug
    D. The Whistler

9. **What instrument does Hans play?**
    A. guitar
    B. trumpet
    C. accordion
    D. tuba

10. **How many races does Rudy win at the Hitler Youth carnival?**
    A. 1
    B. 2
    C. 3
    D. 4

11. **What is Hitler's birthday?**
    A. March 18, 1899
    B. April 20, 1889
    C. August 10, 1880
    D. January 5, 1877

12. **Which of these characters is NOT one of the young thieves?**
    A. Andy Schmeikl
    B. Otto Sturm
    C. Arthur Berg
    D. Fritz Hammer

13. **What are Liesel's nightmares about?**
   A. Hans' death
   B. Max's death
   C. Her father's death
   D. Her brother's death

14. **What is the name of the river where Rudy retrieves Liesel's book?**
   A. Ansler
   B. Seit
   C. Amper
   D. Volga

15. **Which of these does Liesel or Rudy NOT take from the mayor's home?**
   A. The Duden Dictionary
   B. a basket of food
   C. a plate of cookies
   D. The Whistler

16. **Who takes Liesel into their home after the air raid kills Hans and Rosa?**
   A. Walter Kugler
   B. Max Vandenberg
   C. Ilsa Hermann
   D. Alex Steiner

17. **In World War I, who volunteers Hans for a writing assignment?**
   A. Boris Schipper
   B. Erik Vandenburg
   C. Reinhold Zucker
   D. Stephan Schneider

18. **Which of these characters dies in Russia?**
   A. Hans Hubermann
   B. Max Vandenburg
   C. Robert Holtzapfel
   D. Michael Holtzapfel

19. **What game are the Steiner children playing when the Nazis try to take Rudy?**
    A. soccer
    B. dominoes
    C. cards
    D. chess

20. **What does "Himmel" mean in English?**
    A. heaven
    B. hammer
    C. home
    D. hope

21. **Who beats up Ludwig Schmeikl?**
    A. Viktor Chemmel
    B. Liesel Meminger
    C. Rudy Steiner
    D. Tommy Muller

22. **What year does World War II end?**
    A. 1943
    B. 1944
    C. 1945
    D. 1947

23. **Which concentration camp is Max sent to?**
    A. Drancy
    B. Auschwitz
    C. Buchenwald
    D. Dachau

24. **Which city is Molching closest to?**
    A. Berlin
    B. Munich
    C. Cologne
    D. Stalingrad

25. **Where does Liesel die?**

    A. Berlin

    B. Sydney

    C. Molching

    D. Dachau

Quiz 1 Answer Key

1. **(A)** Silver
2. **(C)** The Grave-Digger's Handbook
3. **(A)** Poland
4. **(C)** Cologne
5. **(D)** Stalingrad
6. **(C)** Ilsa Hermann
7. **(B)** The Fiedlers'
8. **(B)** The Standover Man
9. **(C)** accordion
10. **(C)** 3
11. **(B)** April 20, 1889
12. **(B)** Otto Sturm
13. **(D)** Her brother's death
14. **(C)** Amper
15. **(B)** a basket of food
16. **(C)** Ilsa Hermann
17. **(B)** Erik Vandenburg
18. **(C)** Robert Holtzapfel
19. **(B)** dominoes
20. **(A)** heaven
21. **(B)** Liesel Meminger
22. **(C)** 1945
23. **(D)** Dachau
24. **(B)** Munich
25. **(B)** Sydney

Quiz 2

1. **What is the name of the Hitler Youth leader whom Rudy hates?**
    A. Viktor Chemmel
    B. Franz Deutscher
    C. Arthur Berg
    D. Fritz Hammer

2. **Whom does Rudy idolize?**
    A. Hans Hubermann
    B. Viktor Chemmel
    C. Jesse Owens
    D. Adolf Hitler

3. **Which neighbor does Rosa feud with?**
    A. Frau Holtzapfel
    B. Pfiffikus
    C. Frau Diller
    D. Frau Hermann

4. **Which book does Hans Junior say Liesel should be reading?**
    A. Mein Kampf
    B. The Standover Man
    C. The Shoulder Shrug
    D. The Whistler

5. **Which book does Liesel read to Frau Holtzapfel?**
    A. The Word Shaker
    B. Mein Kampf
    C. The Shoulder Shrug
    D. The Whistler

6. **What does Rudy attempt to steal from Mamer's store?**
    A. an apple
    B. an onion
    C. a potato
    D. a book

7. **Which of these is NOT a present Liesel gives to Max?**
   A. a radio
   B. a candy wrapper
   C. a newspaper
   D. a toy soldier

8. **What does Rudy give the pilot?**
   A. a pillow
   B. a teddy bear
   C. a book
   D. water

9. **Which book does Liesel steal from the book burning?**
   A. The Shoulder Shrug
   B. The Grave-Digger's Handbook
   C. Faust the Dog
   D. The Whistler

10. **Who witnesses Liesel steal from the book burning?**
    A. Hans Hubermann
    B. The mayor
    C. Ilsa Hermann
    D. Alex Steiner

11. **Whom do Rudy and Liesel knock off his bicycle to rob?**
    A. Ludwig Schmeikl
    B. Franz Deutscher
    C. Otto Sturm
    D. Fritz Hammer

12. **Which fruit is Rudy's hair color compared to?**
    A. orange
    B. peach
    C. apple
    D. lemon

13. Whom does Max want to cut his hair?

A. Liesel

B. himself

C. Hans

D. Rosa

14. What does Max say he is training for physically?

A. fleeing the country

B. fighting Hitler

C. his health

D. forced labor

15. Which of these is NOT one of Rudy's "three acts of stupidity?"

A. throwing a rock at Franz Deutscher

B. kissing Liesel

C. stealing from Mamer's grocery

D. skipping Hitler Youth meetings

16. What beverage does Liesel say she will never drink again?

A. champagne

B. beer

C. wine

D. vodka

17. Inside which book does Ilsa leave a note for Liesel?

A. The Duden Dictionary

B. The Dream Carrier

C. The Shoulder Shrug

D. The Whistler

18. What does Frau Holtzapfel offer to do if Liesel agrees to read to her?

A. not turn Max into the authorities

B. stop spitting on Rosa's door

C. the Hubermanns' laundry

D. give up her spot in the air raid shelter

19. What does Hans give to an old Jew?

A. his coat

B. champagne

C. bread

D. water

20. Why does Max leave the Hubermanns' home?

A. because Hans thinks the Gestapo will search them

B. because he wants to flee the country

C. because of the air raids

D. because Rosa forces him to

21. Why do the Nazis in trenchcoats want to take Rudy?

A. because he is obedient

B. because he is athletic

C. because he is a Jew

D. because he wants to join the Army

22. Why is Hans' application to the Nazi Party accepted?

A. because he buys a copy of Mein Kampf

B. because he has proven his loyalty to Hitler

C. because the Nazis want to conscript him

D. None of these: Hans' application is never accepted

23. Who is drafted along with Hans?

A. Franz Deutscher

B. Alex Steiner

C. Rudy Steiner

D. Kurt Steiner

24. Where does Hans play the accordion for money?

A. The Amper

B. The Ankler

C. The Kugler

D. The Knoller

25. What is Hans' profession?
A. grocer
B. tailor
C. writer
D. painter

Quiz 2 Answer Key

1. **(B)** Franz Deutscher
2. **(C)** Jesse Owens
3. **(A)** Frau Holtzapfel
4. **(A)** Mein Kampf
5. **(D)** The Whistler
6. **(C)** a potato
7. **(A)** a radio
8. **(B)** a teddy bear
9. **(A)** The Shoulder Shrug
10. **(C)** Ilsa Hermann
11. **(C)** Otto Sturm
12. **(D)** lemon
13. **(A)** Liesel
14. **(B)** fighting Hitler
15. **(B)** kissing Liesel
16. **(A)** champagne
17. **(A)** The Duden Dictionary
18. **(B)** stop spitting on Rosa's door
19. **(C)** bread
20. **(A)** because Hans thinks the Gestapo will search them
21. **(B)** because he is athletic
22. **(C)** because the Nazis want to conscript him
23. **(B)** Alex Steiner
24. **(D)** The Knoller
25. **(D)** painter

Quiz 3

1. **What is Alex Steiner's profession?**
   A. tailor
   B. doctor
   C. teacher
   D. police officer

2. **Which of these is NOT one of the duties of the Air Raid Special Unit?**
   A. propping up buildings
   B. rescuing people
   C. playing air raid sirens
   D. putting out fires

3. **In "The Standover Man," who is the FIRST "standover man?"**
   A. Liesel
   B. Hitler
   C. the father
   D. the fighter

4. **What happens at the end of "The Word Shaker?"**
   A. the tree continues to grow
   B. the tree falls
   C. the tree destroys all of the Fuhrer's trees
   D. None of these

5. **What is Liesel's Christmas gift to Rudy?**
   A. an apple
   B. a navy blue suit
   C. a book
   D. a kiss

6. **Who accuses Hans of cheating at cards?**
   A. Boris Schipper
   B. Erik Vandenburg
   C. Franz Deutscher
   D. Reinhold Zucker

7. **Which part of Michael Holtzapfel's body is severely injured?**
    A. his leg
    B. his ear
    C. his hand
    D. his foot

8. **Who tells Rosa that he heard Hans Junior is alive?**
    A. Max Vandenberg
    B. Hans Senior
    C. Ilsa Hermann
    D. Michael Holtzapfel

9. **Who gives Liesel a blank book?**
    A. Max Vandenberg
    B. Hans Hubermann
    C. Ilsa Hermann
    D. Rudy Steiner

10. **Why does Rudy take a teddy bear to commit burglary?**
    A. for luck
    B. to calm a kid, should he encounter one
    C. to hide stolen goods in
    D. because it reminds him of Liesel

11. **After being dismissed from the Air Raid Special Unit, where is Hans' next military assignment?**
    A. at an airfield
    B. on a submarine
    C. in an office
    D. on the Eastern Front

12. **Why does Michael Holtzapfel kill himself?**
    A. he is terminally ill
    B. he feels guilty about his brother's death
    C. he does not want to see Germany lose the war
    D. his injury is too painful

13. **Who restrains Liesel from going after Max and the rest of the Jews?**
    A. Hans Hubermann
    B. Franz Deutscher
    C. Rudy Steiner
    D. Tommy Muller

14. **When does Liesel kiss Rudy?**
    A. when she gives Rudy the suit
    B. when Rudy retrieves her book
    C. when Rudy is dead
    D. when Rudy is beaten up by Franz Deutscher

15. **What is the name of the book Liesel writes?**
    A. The Word Shaker
    B. The Standover Man
    C. The Whistler
    D. The Book Thief

16. **Of these, when does Death NOT encounter Liesel?**
    A. when Hans and Rosa die
    B. when Liesel's mother dies
    C. when the pilot dies
    D. when Liesel's brother dies

17. **After the bombing raid, what is the only thing Liesel keeps from the Hubermanns' destroyed home?**
    A. Hans' accordion
    B. her book
    C. Rudy's gold medals
    D. her jewelry

18. **What does Death tell Liesel in the end?**
    A. about beauty and brutality
    B. that Death constantly overestimates and underestimates humanity
    C. that Death is haunted by humans
    D. that she is going to Heaven

19. **What does Death need to be distracted from?**
    A. survivors
    B. guns
    C. Nazis
    D. blood

20. **What does Liesel dream of on the train to Munich?**
    A. Hitler
    B. the war
    C. Max
    D. her brother's death

21. **Who coaxes Liesel out of the car when she arrives at the Hubermanns'?**
    A. the foster care agent
    B. Ilsa
    C. Hans
    D. Rosa

22. **Which of these accurately describes Liesel's father?**
    A. a Fascist
    B. a Russian
    C. a Jew
    D. a Communist

23. **Which of these do the Hubermanns' NOT do for money?**
    A. playing music
    B. laundry
    C. painting
    D. tailoring

24. **Who teaches Liesel the alphabet?**
    A. Hans Hubermann
    B. Ilsa Hermann
    C. Sister Maria
    D. Rudy Steiner

25. **What is a "watschen?"**
    A. a beating
    B. a delivery
    C. a coat
    D. a book

Quiz 3 Answer Key

   1. **(A)** tailor
   2. **(C)** playing air raid sirens
   3. **(C)** the father
   4. **(B)** the tree falls
   5. **(B)** a navy blue suit
   6. **(D)** Reinhold Zucker
   7. **(C)** his hand
   8. **(D)** Michael Holtzapfel
   9. **(C)** Ilsa Hermann
 10. **(B)** to calm a kid, should he encounter one
 11. **(C)** in an office
 12. **(B)** he feels guilty about his brother's death
 13. **(C)** Rudy Steiner
 14. **(C)** when Rudy is dead
 15. **(D)** The Book Thief
 16. **(B)** when Liesel's mother dies
 17. **(A)** Hans' accordion
 18. **(C)** that Death is haunted by humans
 19. **(A)** survivors
 20. **(A)** Hitler
 21. **(C)** Hans
 22. **(D)** a Communist
 23. **(D)** tailoring
 24. **(A)** Hans Hubermann
 25. **(A)** a beating

Quiz 4

1. **Why is "The Shoulder Shrug" banned by the Nazis?**
   A. because it was written by a Jew
   B. because it was written by a Communist
   C. because its protagonist is a Jew
   D. because it insults Hitler

2. **How does Hans pay for the two books he gets Liesel on Christmas 1939?**
   A. by trading his cigarette rations
   B. by dipping into his savings
   C. by painting the bookseller's house
   D. by playing the accordion

3. **Who is Rosa's last laundry customer?**
   A. Barbara Steiner
   B. Frau Holtzapfel
   C. Frau Diller
   D. Ilsa Hermann

4. **The book burning is held to mark what occasion?**
   A. the anniversary of Hitler's rise to power
   B. Kristallnacht
   C. Hitler's birthday
   D. Germany's victory in the Battle of Stalingrad

5. **Whom does Liesel pull to safety at the book burning?**
   A. Ludwig Schmeikl
   B. Otto Sturm
   C. Rudy Steiner
   D. Tommy Muller

6. **What does Hans do when Liesel tells him she hates Hitler?**
   A. agree with her
   B. slap her
   C. ground her
   D. report her to the Gestapo

7. **What does Hans buy from the Nazi Party office?**
   - A. nothing
   - B. a photo of Hitler
   - C. a Nazi flag
   - D. a copy of Mein Kampf

8. **Who helps Max escape to Hans Hubermann's home?**
   - A. Walter Kugler
   - B. Liesel Meminger
   - C. Alex Steiner
   - D. Sister Maria

9. **What year does Ilsa's son die?**
   - A. 1918
   - B. 1933
   - C. 1939
   - D. 1944

10. **What year does Hitler take power in Germany?**
    - A. 1918
    - B. 1933
    - C. 1935
    - D. 1939

11. **What does Arthur Berg give Rudy and Liesel just before he leaves Molching?**
    - A. nothing
    - B. a bag of chestnuts
    - C. some apples
    - D. money

12. **How many Jews died in the Holocaust?**
    - A. 6 million
    - B. 12 million
    - C. 60 million
    - D. 600,000

13. Why does Liesel insult the mayor's wife?
   A. because the mayor's wife has turned Liesel in for stealing books
   B. because Liesel is angry about the Holocaust
   C. because the mayor's wife refuses to let Liesel read in her library
   D. because the mayor's wife has fired Rosa

14. Which book does Liesel read to Max?
   A. The Dream Carrier
   B. The Shoulder Shrug
   C. The Grave-Digger's Handbook
   D. The Whistler

15. Which book does Hans read to Liesel?
   A. The Duden Dictionary
   B. The Standover Man
   C. The Grave-Digger's Handbook
   D. The Whistler

16. Which book does Liesel read in the air raid shelter?
   A. The Word Shaker
   B. The Dream Carrier
   C. The Shoulder Shrug
   D. The Whistler

17. When Liesel starts playing soccer, which position does she initially play?
   A. goalie
   B. forward
   C. defender
   D. midfielder

18. What does Hans do the night before he is to leave for the military?
   A. stays awake all night
   B. gets drunk
   C. talks to Max
   D. tries to flee

19. **Why do the Nazis inspect the Hubermanns' basement?**
    A. because they have the wrong address
    B. to see if the Hubermanns own any banned literature
    C. to see if it can be used as a bomb shelter
    D. to see if there are any Jews hidden there

20. **Which of these does Max NOT do in the Hubermanns' basement?**
    A. read the paper
    B. exercise
    C. try to kill himself
    D. write

21. **What does "Mein Kampf" mean in English?**
    A. My Army
    B. My Country
    C. My Struggle
    D. My Life

22. **Which of these characters does NOT give bread to Jews?**
    A. Liesel
    B. Ilsa
    C. Hans
    D. Rudy

23. **Why does Tommy Muller have trouble following marching orders in the Hitler Youth?**
    A. because he does not pay attention
    B. because he has difficulty hearing
    C. because he is insolent
    D. because he has a hip injury

24. **What does Max do during the first air raid?**
    A. Hide in the basement the entire time
    B. Go to the air raid shelter
    C. Light a fire
    D. Look out the window

25. What are Max's nightmares about?
   A. being in a concentration camp
   B. losing a boxing match to Hitler
   C. his father's death
   D. leaving his family

Quiz 4 Answer Key

1. **(C)** because its protagonist is a Jew
2. **(A)** by trading his cigarette rations
3. **(D)** Ilsa Hermann
4. **(C)** Hitler's birthday
5. **(A)** Ludwig Schmeikl
6. **(B)** slap her
7. **(D)** a copy of Mein Kampf
8. **(A)** Walter Kugler
9. **(A)** 1918
10. **(B)** 1933
11. **(B)** a bag of chestnuts
12. **(A)** 6 million
13. **(D)** because the mayor's wife has fired Rosa
14. **(D)** The Whistler
15. **(C)** The Grave-Digger's Handbook
16. **(D)** The Whistler
17. **(A)** goalie
18. **(B)** gets drunk
19. **(C)** to see if it can be used as a bomb shelter
20. **(C)** try to kill himself
21. **(C)** My Struggle
22. **(B)** Ilsa
23. **(B)** because he has difficulty hearing
24. **(D)** Look out the window
25. **(D)** leaving his family

Quiz 5

1. **When was The Book Thief originally published?**
   A. 1955
   B. 1974
   C. 1995
   D. 2005

Quiz 5 Answer Key

1. **(D)** 2005

ClassicNotes

GradeSaver™

Getting you the grade since 1999™

Other ClassicNotes from GradeSaver™

For our full list of over 250 Study Guides, Quizzes,
Sample College Application Essays, Literature Essays and E-texts, visit:

www.gradesaver.com

ClassicNotes

GradeSaver™

Getting you the grade since 1999™

For our full list of over 250 Study Guides, Quizzes,
Sample College Application Essays, Literature Essays and E-texts, visit:

www.gradesaver.com

ClassicNotes

GradeSaver™

Getting you the grade since 1999™

Other ClassicNotes from GradeSaver™

Lolita
Long Day's Journey Into
  Night
Lord Jim
Lord of the Flies
The Lord of the Rings:
  The Fellowship of the
  Ring
The Lord of the Rings:
  The Return of the
  King
The Lord of the Rings:
  The Two Towers
A Lost Lady
The Lottery and Other
  Stories
Love in the Time of
  Cholera
The Love Song of J.
  Alfred Prufrock
Lucy
Macbeth
Madame Bovary
Manhattan Transfer
Mansfield Park
The Master and
  Margarita
MAUS
The Mayor of
  Casterbridge
Measure for Measure
Medea
Merchant of Venice
Metamorphoses
The Metamorphosis
Middlemarch

A Midsummer Night's
  Dream
Moby Dick
Moll Flanders
Mother Courage and Her
  Children
Mrs. Dalloway
Much Ado About
  Nothing
My Antonia
Mythology
Native Son
Nickel and Dimed: On
  (Not) Getting By in
  America
Night
Nine Stories
No Exit
Notes from Underground
O Pioneers
The Odyssey
Oedipus Rex or Oedipus
  the King
Of Mice and Men
The Old Man and the Sea
Oliver Twist
On Liberty
On the Road
One Day in the Life of
  Ivan Denisovich
One Flew Over the
  Cuckoo's Nest
One Hundred Years of
  Solitude
Oroonoko
Othello

Our Town
The Outsiders
Pale Fire
Paradise Lost
A Passage to India
The Pearl
Persuasion
Phaedra
Phaedrus
The Piano Lesson
The Picture of Dorian
  Gray
Poe's Poetry
Poe's Short Stories
Poems of W.B. Yeats:
  The Rose
Poems of W.B. Yeats:
  The Tower
The Poetry of Robert
  Frost
The Poisonwood Bible
Portrait of the Artist as a
  Young Man
Pride and Prejudice
The Prince
Prometheus Bound
Pudd'nhead Wilson
Pygmalion
Rabbit, Run
A Raisin in the Sun
The Real Life of
  Sebastian Knight
The Red Badge of
  Courage
The Remains of the Day
The Republic

For our full list of over 250 Study Guides, Quizzes,
Sample College Application Essays, Literature Essays and E-texts, visit:

www.gradesaver.com

ClassicNotes

GradeSaver™
Getting you the grade since 1999™